D1004530

Of the Beautiful and Sublime

Immanuel
KANT

Observations on the Feeling
of the Beautiful and Sublime

Translated by
JOHN T. GOLDTHWAIT

UNIVERSITY OF CALIFORNIA PRESS
Berkeley, Los Angeles, London

UNIVERSITY OF CALIFORNIA PRESS
Berkeley and Los Angeles, California
UNIVERSITY OF CALIFORNIA PRESS, LTD.
London, England
© 1960 by The Regents of the University of California
California Library Reprint Series Edition 1981
New Paperback Printing 1991
ISBN 0-520-07404-1 (alk. paper)
Library of Congress Catalog Card Number: 60-14379
Designed by Rita Carroll
Printed in the United States of America

4   5   6   7   8   9

The paper used in this publication meets the minimum
requirements of American National Standard for
Information Sciences—Permanence of Paper for Printed
Library Materials, ANSI Z39.48–1984. ⊗

TO

Marguerite Beck, Miriam Bulger,
C. Ada Patterson, and the
memory of Helen Zahniser

Contents

Preface

MY DEBTS TO OTHERS in the preparation of this translation go back more than two decades, to the four ladies whose names appear on the page of dedication. It was they who first opened for me the doors to foreign literatures. I am sure that in dedicating this volume to these teachers of Latin, French, and German, I am but a spokesman for the thousands who have been enriched by their excellent instruction and warmed by their friendship.

I am grateful to Douglas N. Morgan, now of the University of Texas and formerly of Northwestern University, for the suggestion to undertake this translation. Barbara Hoermann of Davis supplied many good English readings of difficult German phrases. I feel a particular debt to Karl Aschenbrenner, whose many specific renditions not only were valuable in themselves but served as examples of the right degree of formality to strike in setting the style of the whole. No doubt the work exhibits many faults, the responsibility for which rests with none of those I have named but with myself alone. If the scholar desires greater exactness or the literary reader greater polish, I hope this effort will stimulate him to improve upon it.

The greatest debt of all is for the patience and forbearance of my wife, Betty Goldthwait, and my son Christopher, during the entire trying period of the preparation of the book.

John T. Goldthwait

Davis, California
December, 1959

Translator's Introduction

IMMANUEL KANT is known largely for the three great works that each bear the name of *Critique*—that is, the *Critique of Pure Reason* of 1781, the *Critique of Practical Reason* of 1788, and the *Critique of Judgment* of 1790. Because of the intent of each volume, signaled by the word *Critique* in each title, the doctrine of these books is called Kant's Critical philosophy. The first of them was published when the author was fifty-eight years of age. All of Kant's works appearing before the first of the Critiques are called his *pre-Critical* writings, perhaps an unfortunate term if it has seemed to judge adversely of their worth. Since this pre-Critical period extended for roughly forty of Kant's most active years, we are justified, I think, in being curious about what was going on in his mind all that time. The book that is the epitome of Kant's pre-Critical thought has the title, *Observations on the Feeling of the Beautiful and Sublime*.[1]

One of the techniques of literary criticism is to refer to the biography of an author in order to come to an understanding of his writings. Factual data concerning his life are thought to be of great, if not necessarily definitive, aid in apprehending the true nature and worth of his message. This technique is shunned by scholars of philosophy, or at least so they profess, since not the man but the thought is what is important. Yet we are all familiar with the accounts of the lives of the great philosophers which are reproduced in the histories of philosophy, and we generally concede their value in enlivening the subject matter of philosophy for the classroom student who does not as yet perceive the relevance of the problems or solutions of philosophy at first sight.

In many of these biographic accounts we derive a commonly held picture of the chief luminary of the German Enlightenment, Immanuel Kant. He is a little man, stooped and stunted by a deformity from birth. He is a bachelor, and is not known ever to have had a love affair. He shuns any intimacy with women, and does not see even his own sister from year's end to year's end. He lives in a house purchased with the savings scrimped together through many years of austere living. He is unemotional; he indulges in no vices nor luxuries. Having been brought up in strict piety, he has not the capacity for the trivial pleasures of the fancy or the imagination. He is known for punctuality in his regimen, serving neighboring housewives as a timepiece with his regular departures for his lecture hall or his constitutional walk. He is the most eminent figure in the University of Königsberg. He has achieved renown throughout Germany. His philosophy has been published not only in several lesser works but in the great Critical trilogy, the *Critique of Pure Reason* on the nature of knowledge, the *Critique of Practical Reason* on ethics, and the *Critique of Judgment* on aesthetics and teleology. He is a great intellect, the first man to elucidate a Categorical Imperative from the dictates of the reason; and he is a stern moralist who can achieve the rare self-discipline necessary to live up to its unrelenting obligation. In a word, we picture what the Germans call a *Verstandesmensch,* a man who lives rigidly according to reason.

Such is the usual characterization of Immanuel Kant. It is, I believe, often conjured up, justly or unjustly, to introduce the beginning student to the Kantian philosophy. Perhaps it is regarded as an aid in inculcating an appreciation of the necessity and of the universality of the characteristic Kantian concept of moral obligation, the Categorical Imperative. Perhaps it is offered as an apology for the unreadable style of Kant's books! One wonders, however, if such an impression of the man's life might not lead toward an inaccurate understanding of Kant's thought by the student, and for that matter, by the teacher who entertains it year after year. I shall maintain here that although the statements given to paint this picture are accurate enough in themselves, they present biographically only a half-truth, representing only half the subject's life. A familiarity with Kant's early maturity and with the works produced in the earlier part of his productive period will lead us to a more attractive portrait. Then having a more adequate knowledge of our man and his work, we shall approach closer to a full understanding of his doctrine. But first a hasty characterization of the mature philosophy against which we shall contrast the earlier thought of its author.

The three *Critiques,* or in other words the Critical philosophy of Kant, are strongly rationalistic in tone. The theme of the whole is the examination of the mind by itself. Kant wanted to know about the mind whatever could be known *a priori*—that is, without recourse to specific experiences. He felt it necessary therefore to write in an extremely dry and abstract style, to prevent the departure of reason from the true pathway through the temptation of feeling. Reason itself must be the instrument with which to demonstrate the limits beyond which reason must not attempt to go. Reason was the guarantor of the Categorical Imperative, the very apex of the Critical philosophy, which commands the individual to act only according to a policy that could be a basis for action by every human being. At a time when some rationalists felt that Kant was destroying rationalism, he had arrived at a positive rationalistic moral teaching, with an economy of presuppositions and a simplicity of deduction which the rationalists more than anyone else could be expected to admire. Finally, even aesthetic experience depended upon the functioning of two of the intellectual faculties, the imagination and the understanding. Its distinguishing characteristic was that the aesthetic pleasure is *disinterested,* not a satisfaction depending on the actual existence of the pleasant object, as, for example, the satisfaction of one's hunger depends upon the actual eating of the food in which one takes delight. Furthermore, since the aesthetic satisfaction depends on the harmony of two of the intellectual faculties, one of which is free in its function, the judgment of the *beauty* of an object is subjective; whereas judgments of its color and shape and other such attributes are objective. This subjectivity was the dominant feature of the Critical aesthetic, and for Kant to have grounded it in reason and intellect was immediately recognized as the most remarkable feature of a remarkable new philosophy of beauty.

The *Critique of Judgment* is so full of aesthetic insights and accurate characterizations of artistic and aesthetic experience that it is proclaimed a wonder Kant ever could have written it when his own life was absolutely and entirely devoid of contact with the arts! This latter statement is substantially true in respect to painting and sculpture, substantially false in respect to drama and literature.

Now we have a brief impression of the mature man and the mature philosophy. What kind of man, and what kind of thought, came before and developed into the sage of Königsberg?

Kant in youth was a classics scholar. During his young manhood, he became a scientist and philosopher. Among the earlier courses he gave in the University of Königsberg were physical geography and anthropology as well as ethics and logic. He published books and papers on strictly scientific topics as well as philosophical ones. His pre-Critical works show his varied interests, his early emphasis on science. Before producing the *Critique of Pure Reason,* he had written twelve treatises in philosophy; but he had also written ten in the physical sciences and two in anthropology, as well as one in education. These works included two on force, motion, and rest, one on combustion, two on the motions of the earth, one on the origin of winds, and three on earthquakes; and most notably the long, erudite and highly original work of 1755, *General Natural History and Theory of the Heavens*. This was the book first proposing the nebular hypothesis of the origin of the solar system. I venture to say that if it had appeared in France or England rather than Germany, Kant's reputation would have been established instantly, and would have placed him near the Newton and Kepler whom he so much admired. As it was, it remained for Laplace to make the nebular hypothesis widely known with a book published in France in 1796.

Kant's other works, however, less profound though they were, had brought him some renown in his own country. In 1766 he was appointed to the post of second librarian of the Royal Library in Königsberg, and the letter from the government in Berlin making the appointment referred to him as "the able Kant, made famous by his books." [2] The University of Berlin invited Kant to accept a professorship in poetics. He refused, however, reluctant to substitute a new environment for the familiar one. The students at Königsberg invited him to lecture on German style, feeling that at last they had found a man who could be the arbiter for their newly respectable native language, whose literature was suddenly growing to more than parochial proportions. This invitation Kant also modestly declined.

In the city of Königsberg, Kant was known as "the

beautiful magister," the appellation obviously being suggested by the title of the *Observations on the Feeling of the Beautiful and Sublime*. In the spirit of those who had given Kant this epithet, Herder wrote a tribute thirty years later to the young magister or lecturer of the seventeen-sixties, showing us a popular, sought-after, eligible, warm man who was no stranger to society.

I had the good fortune to know a philosopher, who was my teacher. He was in his best years, and possessed the cheerful vivacity of youth. . . . His open brow, formed for thought, was the seat of undisturbed serenity and joy; language freighted with thought flowed from his lips; wit and humour were at his command; and his instructive lecture was a rich entertainment. In the same spirit with which he investigated Leibnitz, Wolf, Baumgarten, Crusius, and Hume, and traced the laws of Newton, Kepler, and the scientists generally, he examined the writings of Rousseau then appearing, namely his "Emile" and his "Héloise." He placed the true estimate on every physical discovery which came to his notice, and always returned from other studies to an impartial scrutiny of nature and the moral worth of man. He drew the inspiration for his lectures from the history of men, of nations, and of nature, as well as from natural science, mathematics, and his own observations. He was not indifferent to anything worth knowing. No cabal, no sect, no advantage to himself, no ambition, had the least influence over him compared with the development and illustration of the truth. He encouraged, and obliged his hearers, to think for themselves; despotism was foreign to his mind. This man, whom I mention with the highest esteem and gratitude, is Immanuel Kant.[3]

And again Herder speaks of

Kant, altogether the observer of society, altogether the accomplished philosopher. . . . The great and beautiful in man and in human characters, and temperaments and motivations of the sexes, and virtues and finally of national characters;—that is his world, where he finely notices the finest nuances, finely analyzes the most hidden motivations, and finely delineates many a tiny caprice—altogether a philosopher of the sublime and beautiful of humanity! And in this humane philosophy a German Shaftesbury.[4]

This picture of Kant as he looked to others is confirmed and supplemented by evidence of Kant's inner thoughts. We have his own direct statement of his driving desire to sweep away false and temporary views and arrive at ultimate truth in a comment that Kant had written by hand in his own printed copy of the *Observations on the Feeling of the Beautiful and Sublime*. He wrote, "Everything goes past like a river and the changing taste and the various shapes of men make the whole game uncertain and delusive. Where do I find fixed points in nature, which can not be moved by man, and where I can indicate the markers by the shore to which he ought to adhere?"[5] This question exhibits not despair, but profound longing. As his own response to the diversities of human character and belief, which he had set forth so keenly in the *Observations*, it is a significant key to the life and thought of Kant. The Critical philosophy is his result, the goal of his early desire for fixed points, and we know from Kant's statements late in life that he considered he had discovered the truths to which man should adhere, so far as it was in man's power to know them. As we see not only from Herder's statement but also from Kant's writings, his thought continually returned to man and his moral worth; and the fixed points and markers he sought were guides to moral conduct. The focal point of Kant's philosophical career was the supreme moral principle set down in the *Critique of Practical Reason*. The *Critique of Pure Reason* is perhaps more formidable and even more famous, but it served Kant as a preliminary to ethics. In order to know with finality what it was possible to know in ethics, he felt we must first establish the limitations that bear on knowledge itself, knowledge of any sort.

Now let us consider the sources that were influential in molding Kant's thought. It has often been retold that Kant was brought up on the philosophy of Christian Wolff, which was founded upon that of Leibniz. We are not to assume from this that Kant was a Wolffian or a Leibnizian, pure and simple, in his early years. His early writings abound in expressions of Leibnizian rationalism; but they also contain adverse criticisms on smaller points, showing that Kant was by no means uncritical in the use he made of the Leibnizian framework. His very first published work, "Thoughts on the True Estimation of Living Forces" of 1747, written at the age of twenty-three, was undertaken as a corrective of the interpreters of Leibniz, who in Kant's opinion had distorted the doctrine of living force. In it, however, he accuses Leibniz of circular reasoning in his account in the *Theodicée* of what is the ground of the threefold dimension of space. These are early evidences of a mind that weighs and judges, rather than accepting doctrine under the pressure of authority or reputation. Rationalism provided Kant with doctrine that was a starting point for his thought, and with a vocabulary and method. The dependence upon reason itself as a source of knowledge is a clear mark of Kant's rationalistic heritage, along with many other rationalist presuppositions that mark his Critical philosophy.

A second influence upon Kant's early thought is that of empiricism. Indeed, for a time, in the nineteenth and early twentieth centuries, it was asserted that Kant had passed through a period of empiricism before swinging back, like a pendulum, to the rationalism so apparent in the Critiques. However, just as Kant had not accepted as his own doctrine all the teachings of rationalism, neither did he commit himself to empiricism at any time. Rather, the more thoroughly scholars of various viewpoints approach the intellectual biography of Kant, the more apparent it becomes that from the earliest years onward he was always inquiring, open-minded, and benevolently critical of any school of philosophy with which he became acquainted. Although the *Observations* cannot be said to be based on an empirical philosophy, it does share with empiricism a concentration upon the particulars of experience and a use of the method of inductive generalization rather than deduction from first principles.

Still another source of Kant's thought lay in his religious upbringing. His parents belonged to the movement called Pietism, which had grown up in post-Lutheran Germany, a movement that was so to speak a reformation of the reformation. The Pietists were impatient with even the amount of theology and dogma which the orthodox Lutherans had retained from Roman Catholicism, and insisted upon an even more austere religious regimen. They emphasized Bible reading, moral dealing, prayer, and an inward-reaching contact, through the creature, with the Creator himself. Morality was strongly founded upon the God-given nature of man. This insistence upon man's inherent worth was a cornerstone of Kant's thought throughout his life.

A last influence upon Kant's thought may be mentioned, one not classifiable in the terms used heretofore. It is that of a single man, Rousseau. Kant read Rousseau's works avidly, as soon as they appeared in the bookstores of Königsberg, and he gives us direct testimony of their impress. He states that Rousseau made him respect the masses; not the genius alone but all men are necessary to the progress of humankind. It is interesting that the *Observations* was written after Kant had read *Emile*, but nevertheless he ended the little volume with a statement that the secret of the proper education of young world-citizens had not yet been discovered.

Kant lived in a century in which the interplay of ideas had become newly complex. Philosophy was not simply a question of opposing schools of thought squaring off against each other. Communication, learning, and curiosity all had developed to such an extent that this was no longer possible. Kant was one of the first to avail himself of the many sources of thought, the many methods of inquiry, and the many fountains of inspiration which were flourishing. He was the foremost of those who were dedicated to thoroughness, to attention to every possibility, in the attempt to reach ultimate knowledge. Because he would leave no source untapped, no argument unexamined, his thought was long in maturing. He continued his searches through some twenty-five years of mature manhood until the silent period of 1770 to 1781, in which he was threshing out the important problems of the *Critique of Pure Reason.* We can fairly clearly discern the steps Kant passed through in examining first one doctrine, then another, finally synthesizing the disparate elements of the major known philosophies into the Critical philosophy.

The *Observations on the Feeling of the Beautiful and Sublime,* written in 1763, is Kant's only aesthetic work besides the *Critique of Judgment.* It is the one pre-Critical work that richly discloses the personality of the author, whereas the others allow us only occasionally to glimpse his character. Not only in the observations of human nature and the interpretations placed upon them by its author, but actually in its aesthetic substance, this little volume shows the nature of the man himself. More important, it shows the conception of human nature and experience which was the starting place for the Critical philosophy. It is a unified, original synthesis of the various threads already mentioned, enriched with warm and often acute insights into human motives and feelings.

The Kant of the *Observations* was a very different writer from the Kant of the Critiques. It will not be possible to find parallel passages in respect to content, but let us compare the style of the works. First the well-known heavy-footed march of the *Critique of Pure Reason*:

> What we have expounded separately and singly in the preceding section, we shall now present in systematic interconnection. There are three subjective sources of knowledge upon which rests the possibility of experience in general and of knowledge of its objects—*sense, imagination,* and *apperception.* Each of these can be viewed as empirical, namely, in its application to given appearances. But all of them are likewise *a priori* elements or foundations, which make this empirical employment itself possible. *Sense* represents appearances empirically in *perception, imagination* in *association* (and reproduction), *apperception* in the *empirical consciousness* of the identity of the reproduced representations with the appearances whereby they were given, that is, in recognition.
>
> But all perceptions are grounded *a priori* in pure intuition (in time, the form of their inner intuition as representations), association in pure synthesis of imagination, and empirical consciousness in pure apperception, that is, in the thorough-going identity of the self in all possible representations.[6]

Indeed! Is this the product of the man who was urged to

lecture on German style, who disappointed the University of Berlin by declining to teach poetics? Rather, these honors were accorded on the basis of the style evident in the following two paragraphs, from the *Observations*, which also demonstrate some of the aesthetic doctrine I shall try to elucidate in a few moments. Kant wrote:

> Understanding is sublime, wit is beautiful. Courage is sublime and great, artfulness is little but beautiful. Caution, said Cromwell, is a burgomaster's virtue. Veracity and honesty are simple and noble; jest and pleasant flattery are delicate and beautiful. Graciousness is the beauty of virtue. Unselfish zeal to serve is noble; refinement (*politesse*) and courtesy are beautiful. Sublime attributes stimulate esteem, but beautiful ones, love. People in whom especially the feeling for the beautiful rises seek their sincere, steadfast, and earnest friends only in need, but choose jesting, agreeable, and courteous companions for company. There is many a person whom one esteems much too highly to be able to love him. He inspires admiration, but is too far above us to dare approach him with the familiarity of love.
>
> Those in whom both feelings join will find that the emotion of the sublime is stronger than that of the beautiful, but that unless the latter alternates with or accompanies it, it tires and cannot be so long enjoyed. The lively feelings to which the conversation in a select company occasionally rises must dissolve intermittently in cheerful jest, and laughing delights should make a beautiful contrast with the moved, earnest expression, allowing both kinds of feelings to alternate freely. Friendship has mainly the character of the sublime, but love between the sexes, that of

the beautiful. Yet tenderness and deep esteem give the latter a certain dignity and sublimity; on the other hand, gay jest and familiarity heighten the hue of the beautiful in this emotion. *Tragedy* is distinguished from *comedy,* according to my view, chiefly in that in the first the feeling for the sublime is stirred, and in the second, that for the beautiful. In the first are portrayed magnanimous sacrifices for another's welfare, bold resolution in peril, and proven loyalty. There love is sad, fond, and full of respect; the misfortune of others stirs feelings of sympathy in the breast of the spectator and causes his generous heart to beat for the distress of others. He is gently moved, and feels the dignity of his own nature. On the other hand, comedy sets forth delicate intrigues, prodigious entanglements, and wits who know how to extricate themselves, fools who let themselves be shown up, jests and amusing characters. Here love is not sorrowful; it is pleasurable and familiar. Yet just as in other cases, the noble in this also can be united to a certain degree with the beautiful. (Pp. 51–53.)[7]

The difference in style of the two passages quoted is enough, I think, to account for the disappointment of the educated public when the *Critique of Pure Reason,* keenly anticipated for eleven years, at last could be purchased in Königsberg. The content of the two works also is obviously much different. Whereas the *Critique* discusses faculties, the *Observations* describes people. The *Critique* is concerned with cognition alone; the *Observations* is addressed to cognition as integrated with the feelings and manifested in conduct. The method of the *Critique* is analytical; that of the *Observations* is inductive. Whereas the *Critique* admits that the faculties can be known empirically, it discloses them by the transcendental logic; the *Observations,* however, makes its discoveries through keen observation of the human scene.

Under the circumstances, one would wonder whether there can be any philosophy in the *Observations* at all. Of course there is, as there is an underlying philosophy to any work of literature whatever; but it must be hunted out by analysis where it is not told in direct literal statement. Actually, it is easy to discern the assertions and presuppositions which Kant believed, which became a part of the *Observations on the Feeling of the Beautiful and Sublime.* It is not a work *of* philosophy, taking up a position and arguing it as fully as possible; but it is a work that *has* a philosophy, implicit and sometimes explicit, around which the empirical observations are gathered. The assertions that this philosophy contains are of interest not only to see what was current in Kant's time but to see the genesis of his Critical thought and to come to understand it better.

Now let us spell out explicitly the most important beliefs in this little work that is the epitome of Kant's pre-Critical thought.

Kant's treatise consists of four sections. In the first and briefest, he outlines his purpose, sets himself limits, and introduces the two concepts that he treats, the beautiful and the sublime. In the second section, he explains how these characteristics are exhibited by men in general. In the third, he examines them as they appear in the two sexes, and in the last, as in the different nations.

To orient his discussion and establish the limits within which he proposes to work, Kant points out that the kinds and degrees of pleasures engendered by different objects are dissimilar in different men, and are apparently relative to the individual. He then indicates a scale of the quality of pleasures, with coarse sensual pleasures at one end and the finest intellectual delights at the other. The average person does not necessarily find most of his pleasure in the mean of this scale. Rather, all men are fitted to enjoy the coarse pleasures, and presumably do so to some extent. Only some enjoy the pleasures that are next higher above these; very few can ascend to the level of the qualitatively highest and most delicate pleasures. Those pleasant sensations related to sublimity and beauty, however, are not at the upper extremes but rather are in the middle of the scale. To designate them, Kant consistently uses the comparative adjective, calling them *finer* feelings of pleasure. To enjoy the lower pleasures, no cultivation of talent is necessary. Cultivation, however, is requisite for full enjoyment of the finer feelings.

Any joy or happiness has the form of the gratification of an inclination. Such gratification as we actually enjoy, then, we must initially be endowed with the capacity to enjoy. The endowments of men of course are distributed differently; this is how we can account for their differential enjoyments not only of grosser sense pleasures but also of the finer pleasures of beauty and sublimity, and of the finest pleasures to which only a Kepler is susceptible.

The sublime and the beautiful differ essentially in that the sublime arouses awe and admiration, whereas the beautiful arouses joy. The sublime is divided into three kinds, the terrifying sublime, the noble, and the splendid. Kant subdivides the beautiful into the properly beautiful, which is internal as well as external and contains a considerable admixture of the sublime, and the merely pretty, which is outward only. The sublime emerges as an important moral component of the person.

Kant looks at his subject matter under the aspect of the four accepted classifications of the temperaments of men —melancholy, sanguine, choleric, and phlegmatic. He does not claim that the body humors actually cause the different temperaments, merely that there are noticeable types and that the finer feelings correlate with the other characteristics of each type. The melancholy man has a greater proportion of the sublime in his make-up; the sanguine, of the beautiful; the choleric, of the gloss or appearance rather than the substance of sublimity; and the phlegmatic, neither factor to any discernible extent. Very importantly, the interplay of the sublime and the beautiful generates a description of our moral lives, accounting for the various human motivations including the motivation by moral principle.

As between the sexes, the proper blending of the two feelings will include more of the beautiful in woman, the fair sex, and more of the sublime in man, the noble sex. In his own day these characterizations were perfectly well received by the ladies, although in ours the comparisons would be regarded as giving woman an intolerably low value. At any rate, these were emphases and not radical differences, and they did not deprive woman of the quality of sublimity in the fashion in which it is shared by all mankind. Observing the effects of woman's beauty upon man and of man's noble nature upon woman, Kant concludes that the finer feelings serve to improve each of the sexes in its role in marriage, especially by preserving love and esteem when the satisfaction of coarser inclination diminishes. A marriage should make a single moral person, the husband supplying deep understanding and noble qualities, the wife providing the just sensation of a cultivated taste.

Kant proposes an elaborate scheme to explain different national characters, in which the English, Spanish, and Germans embody the sublime, the French and Italians the beautiful. The Dutch were untouched by nature in either regard. The Englishman is melancholy, the Dutchman phlegmatic, and so on. Although the German inclines toward the choleric, time is improving his taste and molding him more in the stamp of the sublime. Kant appraises his own century as one of a just taste in the arts, science, and morality. He utters a hope for the discovery of the secret of education which will enable men to cultivate the finer tastes and maintain a true appreciation of the sublime and the beautiful.

The foregoing is a summary of the *Observations* according to its own order and emphasis. To study the work from the viewpoint of aesthetics, we must add some further beliefs it embodied, sometimes implicitly rather than explicitly. These receive little emphasis and usually no development, but we can add the following statements as part of the pre-Critical aesthetic. The aesthetic experience is a pleasure, yet not a sense pleasure. The aesthetic response is an immediate, intuitive response. Judgments of taste cannot be brought under speculative principles, although moral conduct can be ordered upon principles. The taste, however, and the conduct that arises from its use, can be cultivated and improved with exercise. There is a very close relation between the aesthetic and moral sides of experience. The beautiful and the sublime are aesthetic categories, but since they (the sublime especially) can be attributes of human subjects and since the sensitivities toward them are human sensitivities, they can also be guides to conduct. Genius acts freely in artistic endeavor. On the other hand, nature can give man the standard for his creativity and his conduct. The one governing consideration for the man of principle is a notion at once aesthetic and moral, namely the beauty and dignity of human nature.

The characteristics given thus far emerge simply from a careful reading of the *Observations* itself, without reference to its historical context. They make a unified scheme describing human nature. To estimate its significance and its degree of originality, we must examine it in relation to the stream of thought in its times.

There is an important distinction involved in the way in which Kant arrived at his generalizations about the beautiful and sublime. Kant established the separate conceptions of beautiful and sublime, his basic aesthetic categories, by analyzing the response of the beholder. The rationalists had done something quite different; they had grounded their conceptions upon nature as exemplified in the rules of reason. Now, we do not know precisely whether to assert that Kant was absolutely original in proceeding in the new way or not. In 1747 Dr. John Baillie, a physician in the British military service in Holland, published in London *An Essay on the Sublime* in which he defined the sublime entirely in terms of the response of the spectator. His essay had a very small circulation, however, and it is extremely doubtful that Kant, who did not read English well, had ever read or even heard of it. What is important in this new approach of Kant's, however, is that it is the first instance of subjectivism in his writing; and one of the most important and original features of the aesthetic of the *Critique of Judgment* is its subjectivism. In the *Critique,* the definitions of both beauty and sublimity, developed in all their branches, depend entirely upon the response of the beholder.

An important question in modern aesthetics has been whether beauty itself is objective or subjective. Does it lie in the object, or does it spring up in the mind? We have seen Kant's solution to this question in the Critical philosophy: The beauty seems phenomenally to belong to the object, but actually a feeling of beauty is simply the sign of the harmonious working of certain faculties of the mind when they are attending to a particular object. In the *Observations* Kant still has not studied this problem and arrived at his later analysis, for here he un-

questioningly regards beauty to be inherent in objects
outside the mind. He had already expressed this view
directly in the *Natural History and Theory of the
Heavens:* "It is true that development, form, beauty, and
perfection are relations of the elements and the sub-
stances that constitute the matter of the universe, and
this is perceived in the arrangements which the wisdom of
God adopts at all times." [8] The reality of beauty is the
constant assumption of the *Observations.* It is the objective element against which taste is found to be subjective and to vary from individual to individual. To
whom was Kant indebted for his view that beauty was
objective? To no one in particular, for this was simply
the accepted belief of his times. Rationalists and empiricists alike made the same assumption. Kant's Critical
description of beauty, removing it from the realm of
the phenomenal object, was for its times quite novel.

Again, the rationalists and empiricists were in agreement, on the whole, on the question of what comprised
beauty in an object. Beauty was unity in variety. It was
an order and a harmonious arrangement of parts in
things which exhibited a pleasing multiplicity. The
rationalists could argue for this definition on the grounds
of authority of the ancients and of the principles of right
reason. Kant departed from them in two ways. First,
whereas the emphasis of the rationalists, and also of
empirically minded British writers, was upon the *unity,*
Kant simply asserted in the *Observations,* "Multiplicity
is beautiful." (P. 67.) He does not say that the multiplicity must show forth any degree of unity, and we do not

discern that unity is a necessary part of the examples of beauty he offers us: rustic flower-strewn meadows, valleys with grazing flocks, flower beds, wit, comedy, complaisance, flattery, youth, smallness of stature, affability. Some of these exhibit unity but some do not; it simply was not essential to beauty.

A second respect in which Kant parted company from the rationalists regarding beauty was in the grounds of his assertions about beauty. He gave his generalizations about beautiful things as the deliverances of his own taste or finer feeling. In this sense these "rules" or generalizations were empirical, unlike the *a priori* rules of the rationalists and neoclassicists. Kant's laws of beauty were inductive, not deductive; and they were descriptive, not prescriptive.

We shall need to refer again soon to the emphasis upon the multiple and various nature of beauty; but let us look now at the notion of sublimity. The sublime had been made an aesthetic category by Longinus, a writer of indistinct identity and date from later Roman times. Boileau had revived the sublime, and, bellwether that he was, had managed to make it an important aesthetic question in the seventeenth and eighteenth centuries. The British writers retained substantially the same views of the nature of beauty as the Continental, but it fell to them to develop the notion of the sublime, perhaps because the Continent was too much hampered by the presence of the neoclassicists of France. Now even in the neat, ordered, and regular parts of a poem of which Boileau would approve there might be, he admitted, a wild element, something disordered and irrational, a single blemish or mark like the beauty patch worn by ladies in court against whose blackness the delicacy of their complexions would be enhanced. The British seized upon this wild element, averring that in some beauties there was something different from regularity. They gradually allowed the concept of the sublime to become a catchall for any aesthetic attribute that did not exhibit the tidy regularity called for by neoclassic criticism.

The inflation of this wild, unfettered element gave to the sublime an interesting evolution. Longinus, and later Boileau, considered the sublime to be the lofty style in rhetoric and poetry. John Dennis expanded it to sublime art, art that was the expression of the greatest passion; this was a conception of greater scope than style alone. Shaftesbury and Addison took the sublime "out of the field of literature and applied it to other arts as well as to nature." [9] Now the neoclassicists and the more empirically minded writers agreed in turning to nature for the standard of art, but their conceptions of nature were different. For Boileau, nature was reason itself, and the nature to which art should refer was an ordered, regular nature operating according to clearly defined laws as the expression of the order and harmony of the divine mind. But the nature of the British, and after them that of Rousseau, was "wild" nature, including the irregularity of grand reaches of land and sea, and the chaotic vastness of the skies. For Shaftesbury, the infinite in nature became sublime, of which one was conscious when contemplating the unending expanses of the starry skies; he consequently found infinity in the Creator to be sublime, and likewise the highest virtue was sublime. For Baillie, the vastness of powers of the mind that could contemplate these things was sublime.

Did Kant add anything to the concept of the sublime? Or was there room for any addition, when the concept already included the infinite? Yes; Kant made an addition whose significance would obviously have been great, if it ever had been developed. Kant adds to the content of the concept of the sublime the one element that has always been the most important aesthetic object for man: namely, man himself.

Kant's conception was quite new. It was not that the powers of the mind give some men sublimity, as for Baillie. Not that highest virtue is sublime, as with Shaftesbury, or genius, as with Kant's countryman Moses Mendelssohn. For it is not solely the superior individual who may claim this trait. Shaftesbury, in making highest virtue sublime for its own sake and in assigning sublimity to the deity, was making sublimity unattainable for man. Kant, rather, affirmed that man himself, by his own nature, and universally, exhibits the sublime. The dominating principle of the virtuous life, he asserts, is to be guided by the "feeling of the beauty and the dignity of human nature." This dignity of human nature unifies all mankind, being common to all, and provides the underlying unity beneath the great diversity which Kant the observer notes. Man's dignity is the ground of the judgment that man himself is sublime.

Now we can revert to the point raised earlier about

Kant's conception of beauty as multiplicity. Let us glance at a passage in the *Observations* which distinctly contrasts the conceptions of beauty and sublimity:

> Finer feeling . . . is . . . of two kinds: the feeling of the *sublime* and that of the *beautiful*. The stirring of each is pleasant, but in different ways. The sight of a mountain whose snow-covered peak rises above the clouds, the description of a raging storm, or Milton's portrayal of the infernal kingdom, arouse enjoyment but with horror; on the other hand, the sight of flower-strewn meadows, valleys with winding brooks and covered with grazing flocks, the description of Elysium, or Homer's portrayal of the girdle of Venus, also occasion a pleasant sensation but one that is joyous and smiling. . . . Tall oaks and lonely shadows in a sacred grove are sublime; flower beds, low hedges and trees trimmed in figures are beautiful. Night is sublime, day is beautiful. Temperaments that possess a feeling for the sublime are drawn gradually, by the quiet stillness of a summer evening as the shimmering light of the stars breaks through the brown shadows of night and the lonely moon rises into view, into high feelings of friendship, of disdain for the world, of eternity. The shining day stimulates busy fervor and a feeling of gaiety. The sublime *moves*, the beautiful *charms*. The mien of a man who is undergoing the full feeling of the sublime is earnest, sometimes rigid and astonished. On the other hand the lively sensation of the beautiful proclaims itself through shining cheerfulness in the eyes, through smiling features, and often through audible mirth. . . .

The sublime must always be great; the beautiful can also be small. The sublime must be simple; the

> beautiful can be adorned and ornamented. . . .
> St. Peter's in Rome is splendid; because on its frame,
> which is large and simple, beauty is so distributed,
> for example, gold, mosaic work, and so on, that the
> feeling of the sublime still strikes through with the
> greatest effect; hence the object is called splendid.
> (Pp. 46–49.)

We notice in these remarks several features that are
distinctive about Kant's pre-Critical aesthetic. We had
stated before that Kant saw beauty in the multifarious;
now we notice that he perceives the sublime in the simple
or the unitary. The sublime must be great and simple;
the beautiful can also be small, adorned and ornamented,
and ephemeral. He is supposing that much that has pre-
viously been called beautiful has actually been both
beautiful and sublime. He provides a new term,
splendid, for objects that exhibit both these qualities. In
fact, the old definition of beauty as unity in variety
would apply most aptly to the objects Kant calls splendid.
He is suggesting that some objects have more beauty
than sublimity, perhaps none of the sublime at all; these
are little, decorative, but perhaps trivial objects; and they
stir a pleasure in us which is one of the finer feelings and
has its own distinct nature. Other objects are character-
istically sublime and not beautiful; they may be grand
and simple, somewhat adorned perhaps but not necessarily so; and they too stir in us a finer pleasure, one that
Kant clearly regards as superior in quality to that stirred
by beauty. Kant had moved further, in this treatise of
1763, than anyone else yet had in providing a subjectivistic aesthetic supported by theoretic distinctions.

The splendid is one of Kant's divisions of the sublime; another, which has important consequences also, is the noble. Let us see its role in one of the finest passages of the work:

> . . . true virtue can be grafted only upon principles such that the more general they are, the more sublime and noble it becomes. These principles are not speculative rules, but the consciousness of a feeling that lives in every human breast and extends itself much further than over the particular grounds of compassion and complaisance. I believe that I sum it all up when I say that it is the *feeling of the beauty and the dignity of human nature*. The first is a ground of universal affection, the second of universal esteem; and if this feeling had the greatest perfection in some one human heart, this man would of course love and prize even himself, but only so far as he is one of all those over whom his broadened and noble feeling is spread. Only when one subordinates his own inclination to one so expanded can our charitable impulses be used proportionately and bring about the noble bearing that is the beauty of virtue. (P. 60.)

The *beauty* of human nature, now, stirs affections. The *dignity* of human nature, the sublime element, stirs esteem. When our intuition perceives that these qualities inhere in all men, we respond by extending our affection and esteem toward all. True virtue, virtue that becomes sublime or "noble," consists in acting according to the principle that all men have human dignity and moral worth—a principle that requires the sensitivity to the sublime to perceive. Further, when one actually does respond to human dignity by performing noble acts, he then gains the noble bearing, the *beauty* of virtue, an aesthetic as well as moral quality. Thus, in his conception of the noble sublime, Kant joins together beauty and virtue, joins together aesthetics and ethics. It was by introducing this admixture of the noble, perhaps, that he became able to respect beauty, which had long been regarded, in his culture, as something at least superfluous and trivial if not a downright harmful temptation.

To those familiar with the Critical ethic, possibly the most conspicuous feature of the passage just quoted is the intuitionism it presupposes. It assumes the intuitive recognition of qualities encountered *in experience,* and not at all the rational grounding of a principle that is applicable *a priori.* Even if the Categorical Imperative depends upon a logical intuition, what is assumed here is an entirely different sort of intuition, a moral or aesthetic intuition. Kant has denied here the very thing which he asserts in the Critical ethic as the chief of the fixed points on the shore to which he could turn from the ever-flowing stream of experience; for here he has said, "These principles are not speculative rules, but the consciousness of a feeling that lives in every human breast." And elsewhere in the *Observations* he writes, "We do an injustice to another who does not perceive the worth or the beauty of what moves or delights us, if we rejoin that *he does not understand* it. Here it does not matter so much what the *understanding* comprehends, but what the feeling senses." (P. 72.) Nothing could be clearer here than Kant's awareness of the dif-

ference between his kind of aesthetic and that of his
rationalist forebears. He was consciously striking out in
a new direction from what they had traveled.

What about the British moral sense writers, then—is
Kant indebted to these? Several British philosophers explained moral quality and beauty as distinct properties of
objects which were perceived by a moral sense and a
sense of beauty, separate sense organs as it were, which
operated just as the eye operates to perceive color and
shape, or the ear to hear the sound quality of an object.
But although the *Observations* bears many superficial
similarities to the works of Shaftesbury, Frances Hutcheson, or Lord Kames, this is the crucial point where
similarity must be established in order to claim that he is
indebted to them. And this is precisely the point on
which he differs from them completely. For they had
asserted a *sense* of beauty, not a *feeling* of beauty; in
German, a *Sinn*, not a *Gefühl*. Kant directly states, however, that feeling is not all of a piece. Rather, in the very
intricate state of life, where the emotions are so varied,
feeling appears very diverse. The feeling of beauty or of
sublimity is not therefore a uniform response to all
beauties or sublimities, a simple signal of their presence.
It is rather a particular total complex of feeling which
pervades the whole mind. It is not uniform, but diverse;
it is not localized, but pervading. Kant certainly did more
justice here to the facts of aesthetic perception than the
moral sense writers.

Now we arrive at the crucial question of the ground of
the moral and aesthetic rules or laws, and of the validity

of this ground. Kant had grounded these upon the principle of the beauty and dignity of human nature. Now, there are two uses of the word "principle." A principle of *explanation* is a concept for explaining why things happen; one explains falling bodies or earth satellites by the principle of gravitation. A principle of *conduct* is a command, an imperative, obeyed by the person whom we characterize as being a man of principle. The chief weakness of the *Observations* as a constructive work in ethics or aesthetics is its failure to carry out successfully the attempt to identify a principle of explanation with a principle of conduct. In context, Kant identifies the empirical principle of human worth, intuitively perceived, with the supreme principle of conduct, but offers no reason why they must be one and the same—why the principle must have the force of obligation. Such a principle Kant believed he had found, later, in the Categorical Imperative, which was grounded of course in reason rather than in moral experience. But although we criticize the *Observations* as a failure in ethical theory, we must admit at once that Kant had at the very beginning of the book disclaimed the intention of offering a theoretic work. He was, he said, writing only as an observer, not a philosopher. We may conclude only that as he saw things at the time, morals and aesthetics were united in an intuitionistic structure, but he could offer no underlying reason why this should be so. The *Observations* was a beginning effort to consolidate the data of the inquiry into the supreme principle of conduct.

Although Kant's description of human beauty and

dignity is highly optimistic, he is not deluded about the
little degree to which men are cognizant of these qualities
or motivated by them. He says:

> In view of the weakness of human nature and of
> the little force which the universal moral feeling
> would exercise over most hearts, Providence has
> placed in us as supplements to virtue assisting drives,
> which, as they move some of us even without prin-
> ciples, can also give to others who are ruled by these
> latter a greater thrust and a stronger impulse toward
> beautiful actions. Sympathy and complaisance are
> grounds of beautiful deeds, which would perhaps
> be altogether suppressed by the preponderance of a
> coarser selfishness; but these are not immediate
> grounds of virtue, as we have seen, although because
> they are ennobled by the relationship with it, even
> they gain its name. I can therefore call them *adoptive
> virtues,* but that which rests upon principles, *gen-
> uine virtue.* The former are beautiful and charming;
> the latter alone is sublime and venerable. One calls
> a disposition in which the first feelings rule a *kind
> heart,* and the man of that sort *goodhearted;* on the
> other hand, one rightly denotes the man who is
> virtuous on principle a *noble heart,* and calls him
> alone a *righteous* person. (Pp. 60–61.)

Then Kant proceeds to study the various motivations of
men. He finds that few act according to the principle of
the beauty and dignity of human nature. More act out
of goodhearted impulses. Most men act from self-interest.
Yet there is one motive held in common by all. He writes:

> Finally the *love of honor* has been disseminated
> to *all* men's hearts, although in unlike measure. . . .

For although ambition is a foolish fancy so far as it becomes a rule to which one subordinates the other inclinations, nevertheless as an attendant impulse it is most admirable. For since each one pursues actions on the great stage according to his dominating inclinations, he is moved at the same time by a secret impulse to take a standpoint outside himself in thought, in order to judge the outward propriety of his behavior as it seems in the eyes of the onlooker. Thus the different groups unite into a picture of splendid expression, where amidst great multiplicity unity shines forth, and the whole of moral nature exhibits beauty and dignity. (Pp. 74–75.)

Surely these passages show candid recognition of the true nature of most of men's motives. Yet we see again the union of moral and aesthetic attributes in the concept of the splendid, in which unity and multiplicity are joined; and we see that Kant warmly extends his own affection and esteem to all mankind, who when seen from a universal point of view may fitly be characterized as splendid.

Our last question is the relationship of the *Observations* to Kant's final work in aesthetics, the *Critique of Judgment*. Was this brief, early treatise a precursor of the later one? No, it is not, in the sense that a reader of the *Observations* would not have been able to see what was coming and predict the doctrine of the *Critique*. Kant himself was unable to do this, in 1763. He had no inkling that he would write an aesthetic theory later in life, much less any idea of what it would contain. But

the *Observations* is nevertheless clearly and definitely
related to the *Critique* in Kant's intellectual development, a necessary stage on its author's way to his final
position. It served him as a repository for the data that
a theory of beauty must explain; and served him so well
that he actually drew upon some of its materials almost
verbatim when the twenty-six-year-long period of gesta-
tion came to an end. It also recorded some of the beliefs
that went into the final structure of Kantian aesthetic
theory.

Before listing any similarities between the earlier and
the later aesthetic, we will acknowledge again the
change to which attention has already been drawn; Kant
abandoned the effort to ground the supreme rule of
conduct empirically, correcting the fallacy of attempting
to make such a rule serve in the two capacities of a
principle of explanation and a principle of conduct.
Rather, he grounded the supreme rule of conduct upon
the nature of reason.

His only other change of importance was a qualifica-
tion of the emotion of the sublime. The feeling of the
sublime, he decided, includes fear, a species of pain. Yet
the fear that is present is outweighed by the pleasure that
the soul takes in the discovery of the extent of its own
powers. By this explanation Kant in effect extended the
emotion of his subdivision, the terrifying sublime, to become the emotion of the sublime itself. Possibly Kant
was persuaded to do this by his own further experience,
possibly by Edmund Burke's treatise, *A Philosophical*

Inquiry into the Origin of Our Ideas of the Sublime and Beautiful. Burke had explained the emotion of the sublime as a feeling of fear which grips one in the presence of some mighty object, but then turns to delight when one learns that he is not in actual danger. The ability of the mind to transcend the thought of danger Kant took as a sign of its moral dignity.

What conceptions of the *Observations* does Kant preserve in the *Critique of Judgment?* The list is sufficient to indicate that he had already chosen his direction in aesthetics, even though he had not reached his eventual goal, in the earlier period.

First of all, Kant deals with the same data, the data any theory of beauty must account for. Prominent among them are the great diversity of aesthetic responses and of aesthetic judgments among individuals.

He acknowledges the importance of feeling, but denies that aesthetic response is either simply hedonistic or simply utilitarian. This denial takes the form, in the later work, of the famous doctrine that aesthetic response is a *disinterested* satisfaction. It is made to be a pleasure rising from the inner life of the mind rather than the life of the senses, hence is still in rank a "finer" feeling.

He affirms still that the aesthetic response is active, not passive, and is immediate, not mediated, as though by a sense organ.

He retains the major division of aesthetic experience into responses to the beautiful and responses to the sublime.

Although qualified in the later work as a pleasure rising out of fear, the response to the sublime, like that to the beautiful, is still considered to be a pleasure.

The finer feeling still serves to differentiate the different qualities of different aesthetic objects; that is, it still functions as *taste*.

Taste can be cultivated and improved with exercise.

The subjectivistic approach is not only retained, but developed thoroughly.

Genius is still held to be free. Now, however, it is only the genius, not just any person of taste, who may read and apply the standard by which nature gives the rule to art.

Kant preserves the same content in the two concepts, the beautiful and sublime. The beautiful includes birds, sea shells, articles of dress and furniture, dwellings, trees, gardens, bird song, a summer day, and yes, woman—as well as the products of beautiful art. The sublime objects still include the pyramids of Egypt, St. Peter's Cathedral, the wild greatness of nature, the infinite, mountain peaks, ocean storms, the starry vault, courage, sacrifice, the separation from society when this rises from an idea that overlooks personal interest. In fact, there is a long passage[10] in the *Critique of Judgment,* in which Kant works out the explanations of the sensations of beauty and sublimity, which has so many echoes of the *Observations* that I am convinced he had the earlier book open before him as he wrote this part of the later.

The sublime, as it is retained in the Critical aesthetic, continues to serve the important function it had had in the pre-Critical. That is the uniting of aesthetic with moral experience. Kant continues to affirm that the sublime makes man conscious of his destination, that is, his moral worth. For the feeling of the sublime is really the feeling of our own inner powers, which can outreach in thought the external objects that overwhelm our senses; and prominent among these inner powers is the moral faculty. Moreover, Kant affirms in the *Critique,* indeed at the very conclusion of the part on aesthetics, that "taste is at bottom a faculty for judging of the sensible illustration of moral ideas." [11] Thus both the judgment of the sublime and the judgment of the beautiful remain linked to moral experience.

The present examination has dissected and held up to light some of the features of Kant's early aesthetic, the body of belief he held in his early maturity, which he must either confirm or revise in order to produce a new and significant work in the field. Embodied in this early aesthetic we found an entire outlook upon mankind, an outlook that required its holder to pursue to its final conclusion the search for the ultimate rule of ethics for the edification of the human race, whom he loved and esteemed universally. In the necessity for analysis, perhaps I have drawn emphasis away from one of my theses, which is that Kant was no *Verstandesmensch,* no dry creature of the reason alone. I appeal to the reader to recall the passages quoted from the *Observations.* Better yet, I call upon him to read it and judge. He will become aware of Kant's sensitivity to different shadings of experience, his awareness of the inner nature of men, his humor, gentleness, warmth, his charity toward the many human imperfections that strike the observer on all sides, and his noble respect for the underlying dignity of all humanity. It is because these qualities are added to the considerations of philosophy and science that I accord the *Observations* the chief place among the pre-Critical works, regarded from the standpoint of reflecting truly Kant's mind and grasp. It is these qualities that typify Kant's lifelong outlook upon the world and man; it was these responses that drove him to the search for a firmly grounded ethic, for man's guidance; and it was the need to discover this ethic which motivated the writing of the *Critique of Pure Reason,* to establish whether certain knowledge of such an ethic were possible.

The charge is often made that Kant's formalistic ethic, hinging upon the rationally grounded Categorical Imperative, is heedless of the role of human feeling, indicating that its author was insensitive to the true nature of moral experience. A reading of the *Observations,* however, quickly refutes the accusation of insensitivity in the author, and suggests that a complete understanding of Kantian formalistic ethics takes feeling into account. For these reasons, the teacher of Kant's ethics at least, if not the pupil, should be familiar with the *Observations on the Feeling of the Beautiful and Sublime.*

Notes on the Translation

A TRANSLATION OF KANT's *Beobachtungen über das Gefühl des Schönen und Erhabenen* into English, the only complete translation offered heretofore in this language, was made in London in 1799. It was included in a two-volume set of Kant's shorter works, entitled *Essays and Treatises on Moral, Political and Various Philosophical Subjects by E. Kant*. The first volume appeared in 1798; its title page attributed the work to "the Translator of the Principles of Critical Philosophy," another volume that had appeared anonymously. Creighton and Lefevre give A. F. M. Willich as the translator of the *Essays and Treatises* in their translation of Paulsen's biography,[1] following Duncan's bibliography in *Kant-Studien*.[2] Bayard Quincy Morgan lists the work as that of Willich, also ascribing to him the translation of *Principles of Critical Philosophy*.[3] René Wellek, however, identifies this translator as John Richardson, a young Scotsman who had learned of Kant through a professor of his, a former pupil of Kant's, J. S. Beck of the University of Halle, the author of the *Principles of Critical Philosophy*.[4] Still another suggestion is made by Lewis White Beck as to the translator: "This edition was published by William Richardson in London, and probably is his own trans-

lation." [5] The evidence being so slight and the sugges-
tions so numerous, it seems safest to refer to the work as
that of "the anonymous translator." This translation was
not successful in earning a hearing in England for Kantian philosophy, and so few copies were printed that the
edition is virtually unheard of among students of Kant.
The sole copy in America, to my knowledge, is in the
Harvard College Library.

A more effective propagandist for Kant was Thomas
De Quincey, who translated a few selections from Kant
and discussed Kant's ideas. In De Quincey's *Works* there
appears a translation of section four of the *Observations,*
on national characters, which he published in the *London
Magazine* for April, 1824.[6] In our own century a few
passages of the work have found their way into English.
Many short ones appear in the early chapters of *Kant's
Pre-Critical Ethics* by Paul Arthur Schilpp.[7] In a set of
Kantian selections, Carl J. Friedrich has offered a translation of a few pages of section one and about two-thirds
of section four.[8] Among other languages, translations have
been made in Spanish, Slovene, and French, no less than
five having appeared in the latter language. The first,
attributed to Peyer-Imhoff, appeared in 1796; two versions,
by Auguste Hilarion de Keratry and by M. Veyland,
appeared in 1823; that of J. Barni accompanied his translation of the *Critique of Judgment* in 1846; a well-
annotated and scholarly edition was provided by R.
Kempf in 1953.

I have attempted, of course, to make every prudent use
of the English translations and of the four most recent

French translations. I believe, however, that the following version does not show the stamp of any one of these. The anonymous translation, already in an antiquated English, follows the German too literally to serve as a model of smooth language; and although I claim no great stylistic virtue for the present version, I have tried to keep in mind that Kant was praised for his style in the period in which the *Observations* appeared. The translators of brief passages only have not been confronted with the difficulties inherent in producing a unified and self-consistent version of the whole work. Finally, the problems of translation here are more literary than philosophical, hence more of idiom than of technical exposition, and to work through the medium of a third language is needlessly to multiply the possibilities of deviation from the spirit of the original.

The present translation is an attempt to remain as close as possible to the original work, and to preserve its internal consistency even where this demands a variety of English words for separate occurrences of one German word. The grammatical and rhetorical structures of the two languages being different, it is impossible actually to reproduce the original author's style in translation. The effort has been made, however, to keep the original figures of speech, and to attain smooth and leisurely rather than labored reading. If something of the lightness has been kept with which an eighteenth-century German might have been impressed upon reading the original, the success of the translation will have exceeded my expectations. I have felt, however, that strict observance of the actual original content was paramount, and have preferred to err on the side of heaviness or colorlessness if that were necessary to preserve the author's message.

Kant was generous with mechanical marks of emphasis, having many significant words or quotations set in bold-face or leaded type. Rather than retain all these marks, which are not customary in English, I have italicized words so emphasized only where such a word is first introduced, or where attention should be brought to Kant's use of it in his own special sense, or where the organization of his thought can best be made apparent by that means. Of course, no words have been italicized which were not thus emphasized in the original.

Kant's own notes are indicated by asterisks, and appear as footnotes in the text, as in the original. Notes of the translator are numbered, and collected at the back of the book.

OBSERVATIONS ON THE FEELING OF THE BEAUTIFUL AND SUBLIME

Of the Distinct Objects of the Feeling of the Beautiful and Sublime

THE VARIOUS FEELINGS OF ENJOYMENT or of displeasure rest not so much upon the nature of the external things that arouse them as upon each person's own disposition to be moved by these to pleasure or pain. This accounts for the joy of some people over things that cause aversion in others, or the amorous passion so often a puzzle to everybody, or the lively antipathy one person feels toward something that to another is quite indifferent. The field of observation of these peculiarities of human nature extends very wide, and still conceals a rich source for discoveries that are just as pleasurable as they are instructive. For the present I shall cast my gaze upon only a few places that seem particularly exceptional in this area, and even upon these more with the eye of an observer than of a philosopher.

Because a person finds himself happy only so far as he gratifies an inclination, the feeling that makes him capable of enjoying great pleasures, without needing exceptional talents to do so, is certainly no trifle. Stout persons, whose favorite authors are their cooks and whose works of fine taste are in their cellars, will thrive on vulgar obscenities and on a coarse jest with just as lively a delight as that upon which persons of noble sensitivity pride themselves. An indolent man who loves having books read aloud to him because it is so pleasant to fall asleep that way, the merchant to whom all pleasures are trifling except those a clever man enjoys when he calculates his profits, one who loves the opposite sex only so far as he counts it among things to enjoy, the lover of the hunt, whether he hunt flies like Domitian[1] or ferocious beasts like A. . . . ,—all these have a feeling that makes them capable of enjoying pleasures after their own fashion, without presuming to envy others or even being able so much as to conceive of other pleasures. But to that kind of feeling, which can take place without any thought whatever, I shall here pay no attention. There is still another feeling of a more delicate sort, so described either because one can enjoy it longer without satiation and exhaustion; or because it presupposes a sensitivity of the soul, so to speak, which makes the soul fitted for virtuous impulses; or because it indicates talents and intellectual excellences. It is this feeling of which I wish to consider one aspect. I shall moreover exclude from it that inclination that is fixed upon high intellectual insights, and the thrill that was possible to a Kepler, who, as Bayle reports,[2] would not have sold one of his discoveries for a princedom. The latter sensation is quite too delicate to belong in the present sketch, which will concern only the sensuous feeling of which also more ordinary souls are capable.

Finer feeling, which we now wish to consider, is chiefly of two kinds: the feeling of the *sublime* and that of the *beautiful*. The stirring of each is pleasant, but in different ways. The sight of a mountain whose snow-covered peak rises above the clouds, the description of a raging storm, or Milton's portrayal of the infernal kingdom,[3] arouse enjoyment but with horror; on the other hand, the sight of flower-strewn meadows, valleys with winding brooks and covered with grazing flocks, the description of Elysium,[4] or Homer's portrayal of the girdle of Venus,[5] also occasion a pleasant sensation but one that is joyous and smiling. In order that the former impression could occur to us in due strength, we must have a *feeling of the sublime,* and, in order to enjoy the latter well, a *feeling of the beautiful.* Tall oaks and lonely shadows in a sacred grove are sublime; flower beds, low hedges and trees trimmed in figures are beautiful. Night is sublime, day is beautiful. Temperaments that possess a feeling for the sublime are drawn gradually, by the quiet stillness of a summer evening as the shimmering light of the stars breaks through the brown shadows of night and the lonely moon rises into view, into high feelings of friendship, of disdain for the world, of eternity. The shining day stimulates busy fervor and a feeling of gaiety. The sublime *moves,* the beautiful *charms.* The mien of a man who is undergoing the full feeling of the sublime is earnest, sometimes rigid and astonished. On the other hand the lively sensation of the beautiful proclaims itself through shining cheerfulness in the eyes, through smiling features, and often through audible mirth. The sublime is in turn of different kinds. Its feeling is sometimes accompanied with a certain dread, or melancholy; in some cases merely with quiet wonder; and

in still others with a beauty completely pervading a sublime plan. The first I shall call the *terrifying sublime,*
the second the *noble,* and the third the *splendid.* Deep
loneliness is sublime, but in a way that stirs terror.*
Hence great far-reaching solitudes, like the colossal
Komul Desert in Tartary, have always given us occasion for
peopling them with fearsome spirits, goblins, and ghouls.

The sublime must always be great; the beautiful can
also be small. The sublime must be simple; the beautiful
can be adorned and ornamented. A great height is just
as sublime as a great depth, except that the latter is ac-

---

* I should like to give just one example of the noble awe
that the description of complete loneliness can inspire, and I
draw for that purpose upon some passages from "Carazan's
Dream" in the *Bremen Magazine,* volume IV, page 539. In proportion as his riches increased, this wealthy miser had closed off
his heart from compassion and love toward all others. Meantime,
as the love of man grew cold in him, the diligence of his prayer
and his religious observances increased. After this confession, he
goes on to recount the following: "One evening, as by my lamp
I drew up my accounts and calculated my profits, sleep over-
powered me. In this state I saw the Angel of Death come over
me like a whirlwind. He struck me before I could plead to be
spared his terrible stroke. I was petrified, as I perceived that my
destiny throughout eternity was cast, and that to all the good I
had done nothing could be added, and from all the evil I had
committed, not a thing could be taken away. I was led before
the throne of him who dwells in the third heaven. The glory that
flamed before me spoke to me thus: 'Carazan, your service of
God is rejected. You have closed your heart to the love of man,
and have clutched your treasures with an iron grip. You have
lived only for yourself, and therefore you shall also live the
future in eternity alone and removed from all communion with
the whole of Creation.' At this instant I was swept away by an

companied with the sensation of shuddering, the former with one of wonder. Hence the latter feeling can be the terrifying sublime, and the former the noble. The sight of an Egyptian pyramid, as Hasselquist[6] reports, moves one far more than one can imagine from all the descriptions; but its design is simple and noble. St. Peter's in Rome is splendid; because on its frame, which is large and simple, beauty is so distributed, for example, gold, mosaic work, and so on, that the feeling of the sublime still strikes through with the greatest effect; hence the object is called splendid. An arsenal must be noble and simple, a residence castle splendid, and a pleasure palace beautiful and ornamented.

A long duration is sublime. If it is of time past, then

---

unseen power, and driven through the shining edifice of Creation. I soon left countless worlds behind me. As I neared the outermost end of nature, I saw the shadows of the boundless void sink down into the abyss before me. A fearful kingdom of eternal silence, loneliness, and darkness! Unutterable horror overtook me at this sight. I gradually lost sight of the last star, and finally the last glimmering ray of light was extinguished in outer darkness! The mortal terrors of despair increased with every moment, just as every moment increased my distance from the last inhabited world. I reflected with unbearable anguish that if ten thousand times a thousand years more should have carried me along beyond the bounds of all the universe I would still always be looking ahead into the infinite abyss of darkness, without help or hope of any return—. In this bewilderment I thrust out my hands with such force toward the objects of reality that I awoke. And now I have been taught to esteem mankind; for in that terrifying solitude I would have preferred even the least of those whom in the pride of my fortune I had turned from my door to all the treasures of Golconda—"

it is noble. If it is projected into an incalculable future, then it has something of the fearsome in it. A building of the remotest antiquity is venerable. Haller's description of the coming eternity[7] stimulates a mild horror, and of the past, transfixed wonder.

Of the Attributes of the Beautiful and Sublime in Man in General

UNDERSTANDING IS SUBLIME, wit is beautiful. Courage is sublime and great, artfulness is little but beautiful. Caution, said Cromwell, is a burgomaster's virtue. Veracity and honesty are simple and noble; jest and pleasant flattery are delicate and beautiful. Graciousness is the beauty of virtue. Unselfish zeal to serve is noble; refinement (*politesse*) and courtesy are beautiful. Sublime attributes stimulate esteem, but beautiful ones, love. People in whom especially the feeling for the beautiful rises seek their sincere, steadfast, and earnest friends only in need, but choose jesting, agreeable, and courteous companions for company. There is many a person whom one esteems much too highly to be able to love him. He inspires admiration, but is too far above us for us to dare approach him with the familiarity of love.

Those in whom both feelings join will find that the emotion of the sublime is stronger than that of the beautiful, but that unless the latter alternates with or accompanies it, it tires and cannot be so long enjoyed.* The

* The sensations of the sublime exert the powers of the soul more strongly, and therefore tire sooner. One will be able to read a pastoral poem longer at a time than Milton's *Paradise Lost,* and

lively feelings to which the conversation in a select company occasionally rises must dissolve intermittently in cheerful jest, and laughing delights should make a beautiful contrast with the moved, earnest expression, allowing both kinds of feelings to alternate freely. Friendship has mainly the character of the sublime, but love between the sexes, that of the beautiful. Yet tenderness and deep esteem give the latter a certain dignity and sublimity; on the other hand, gay jest and familiarity heighten the hue of the beautiful in this emotion. *Tragedy* is distinguished from *comedy*, according to my view, chiefly in that in the first the feeling for the sublime is stirred, and in the second, that for the beautiful. In the first are portrayed magnanimous sacrifices for another's welfare, bold resolution in peril, and proven loyalty. There love is sad, fond, and full of respect; the misfortune of others stirs feelings of sympathy in the breast of the spectator and causes his generous heart to beat for the distress of others. He is gently moved, and feels the dignity of his own nature. On the other hand, comedy sets forth delicate intrigues, prodigious entanglements, and wits who know how to extricate themselves, fools who let themselves be shown up, jests and amusing characters. Here love is not sorrowful; it is pleasurable and familiar. Yet just as in other

---

La Bruyère longer than Young. It seems to me to be especially a fault of the latter, as a moral poet, that he too uniformly maintains a sublime tone; for the strength of the impression can be renewed only through interspersing gentler passages. In the beautiful, nothing tires more than laborious craftsmanship which betrays itself there. The effort to charm is experienced as painful and toilsome.

cases, the noble in this also can be united to a certain
degree with the beautiful.

Even depravities and moral failings often bear, for all
that, some features of the sublime or beautiful, at least
so far as they appear to our sensory feeling without being
tested by reason. The anger of someone fearsome is sublime, like Achilles' wrath in the *Iliad*. In general, a hero
of Homer's is the terrifying sublime; one of Vergil's, on
the other hand, is noble. Open bold revenge, following a
great offense, bears something of the great about it; and
as unlawful as it may be, nevertheless its telling moves
one with both horror and gratification. When Shah Nadir
was set upon at night in his tent by some conspirators, as
Hanway[1] reports, after he had already received some
wounds and was defending himself in despair, he cried
out, "Mercy! I will pardon you all!" One among them
answered, as he raised his saber on high, "You have shown
no mercy, and you deserve none." Resolute audacity in a
rogue is of the greatest danger, but it moves in the telling,
and even if he is dragged to a disgraceful death he nevertheless ennobles it to some extent by going to it defiantly
and with disdain. On the other side, a scheme contrived
deceitfully, even when it is bent on some piece of
knavery, has something about it which is delicate, and is
laughed at. The amorous inclination (*coquetterie*) in a
delicate sense, that is, an endeavor to fascinate and charm,
in an otherwise decorous person is perhaps reprehensible
but still beautiful, and usually is set above the respectable,
earnest bearing.

The figure of persons who please by their outward

appearance falls sometimes into one, sometimes into the other sort of feeling. A large stature gains regard and esteem, a small one rather familiarity. In fact, dark coloring and black eyes are more closely related to the sublime, blue eyes and blonde coloring to the beautiful. A somewhat greater age conforms more with the qualities of the sublime, but youth with those of the beautiful. It is the same way with the distinction determined by stations; and in all the points suggested, even the costumes must accord with this distinction of feeling. Great, portly persons must observe simplicity, or at most, splendor, in their apparel; the little can be adorned and embellished. For age, darker colors and uniformity in apparel are seemly; youth radiates through lighter colored and vividly contrasting garments. Among the classes with similar power and rank, the cleric must exhibit the greatest simplicity, the statesman the most splendor. The paramour may adorn himself as he pleases.

There is also something in external circumstances which, at least according to the folly of men, concerns these sensations. High birth and title generally find people bowed in respect. Wealth without merit is honored even by the disinterested, presumably because with its idea we associate projects of great actions which can be carried out by its means. This respect falls occasionally to many a rich scoundrel, who will never perform such actions and has no concept of the noble feeling that alone can make riches valuable. What increases the evil of poverty is contempt, which cannot be completely overcome even by merits, at least not before common eyes,

unless rank and title deceive this coarse feeling and to
some extent impose upon its advantage.

In human nature, praiseworthy qualities never are
found without concurrent variations that must run
through endless shadings to the utmost imperfection. The
quality of the *terrifying sublime,* if it is quite unnatural,
is adventurous.* Unnatural things, so far as the sublime
is supposed in them, although little or none at all may
actually be found, are *grotesque.* Whoever loves and
believes the fantastic is a *visionary;* the inclination toward
whims makes the *crank.* On the other side, if the noble is
completely lacking the feeling of the beautiful degenerates, and one calls it *trifling.* A male person of this
quality, if he is young, is named a *fop;* if he is of middle
age, he is a *dandy.* Since the sublime is most necessary
to the elderly, an *old dandy* is the most contemptible
creature in nature, just as a young crank is the most offen-
sive and intolerable. Jests and liveliness pertain to the
feeling of the beautiful. Nevertheless, much understanding can fittingly shine through, and to that extent they
can be more or less related to the sublime. He in whose
sprightliness this admixture is not detectable *chatters.*
He who perpetually chatters is *silly.* One easily notices
that even clever persons occasionally chatter, and that
not a little intellect is needed to call the understanding
away from its post for a short time without anything going
wrong thereby. He whose words or deeds neither entertain
nor move one is *boring.* The bore, if he is nevertheless

---

* So far as sublimity or beauty exceeds the known average,
one tends to call it *fictitious.*

zealous to do both, is *insipid*. The insipid one, if he is
conceited, is a fool.*

I shall make this curious sketch of human frailties
somewhat more understandable by examples; for he to
whom Hogarth's engraving stylus is wanting must com-
pensate by description for what the drawing lacks in
expression. Bold acceptance of danger for our own, our
country's, or our friends' rights is sublime. The crusades
and ancient knighthood were adventurous; duels, a
wretched remnant of the latter arising from a perverted
concept of chivalry, are grotesque. Melancholy separation
from the bustle of the world due to a legitimate weariness
is noble. Solitary devotion by the ancient hermits was
adventurous. Monasteries and such tombs, to confine the

---

* One soon observes that this praiseworthy company divides
into two compartments, that of the cranks and that of the dandies.
A learned crank is discreetly called a *pedant*. If he assumes an
obstinate appearance of wisdom, like the *dunce* of ancient and
recent times, then the cap with bells becomes him well. The class
of dandies is more often encountered in high society. Perhaps it
is still better than the first. At their expense one has much to
gain and much with which to amuse oneself. For all that, in this
caricature each makes a wry mouth at the other, and knocks with
his empty head on the head of his brother.

[*Dunce:* " 'Duns' or 'Dunsman' was a name early applied by
their opponents to the followers of Duns Scotus, the Scotists, and
hence was equivalent to one devoted to sophistical distinctions
and subtleties. When, in the 16th century, the Scotists obsti-
nately opposed the 'new learning,' the term 'duns' or 'dunce'
became in the mouths of the humanists and reformers, a term of
abuse, a synonym for one incapable of scholarship, a dull block-
head."—"Dunce," *Encyclopaedia Britannica,* 11th ed. (New York,
1910).]

living saints, are grotesque. Subduing one's passions through principles is sublime. Castigation, vows, and other such monks' virtues are grotesque. Holy bones, holy wood, and all similar rubbish, the holy stool of the High Lama of Tibet not excluded, are grotesque. Of the works of wit and fine feeling, the epic poems of Vergil and Klopstock fall into the noble, of Homer and Milton into the adventurous. The *Metamorphoses* of Ovid are grotesque; the fairy tales of French foolishness are the most miserable grotesqueries ever hatched. Anacreontic poems are generally very close to the trifling.

Works of understanding and ingenuity, so far as their objects also contain something for feeling, likewise take some part in the differences now being considered. Mathematical representation of the infinite magnitude of the universe, the meditations of metaphysics upon eternity, Providence, and the immortality of our souls contain a certain sublimity and dignity. On the other hand, philosophy is distorted by many empty subtleties, and the superficial appearance of profundity cannot prevent our regarding the four syllogistic figures as scholastic trifling.[2]

Among moral attributes true virtue alone is sublime. There are nevertheless good moral qualities that are amiable and beautiful, and, so far as they harmonize with virtue, will also be regarded as noble, although they cannot properly be included within the virtuous disposition. The judgment concerning this is subtle and complex. Of course one cannot call that state of mind virtuous

which is a source of such actions as might be grounded
in virtue itself but whose actual cause accords with virtue
only accidentally, and which may often, by its very
nature, conflict with the general rules of virtue. A certain tenderheartedness, which is easily stirred into a warm
feeling of *sympathy,* is beautiful and amiable; for it shows
a charitable interest in the lot of other men, to which
principles of virtue likewise lead. But this good-natured
passion is nevertheless weak and always blind. For sup-
pose that this feeling stirs you to help a needy person
with your expenditure. But you are indebted to another,
and doing this makes it impossible for you to fulfill the
stern duty of justice. Thus the action obviously cannot
spring from a virtuous design; for such could not possibly
induce you to sacrifice a higher obligation to this blind
fascination. On the other hand, when universal affection
toward the human species has become a principle within
you to which you always subordinate your actions, then
love toward the needy one still remains; but now, from a
higher standpoint, it has been placed in its true relation
to your total duty. Universal affection is a ground of
your interest in his plight, but also of the justice by
whose rule you must now forbear this action. Now as
soon as this feeling has arisen to its proper universality, it
has become sublime, but also colder. For it is not possible
that our heart should swell from fondness for every man's
interest and should swim in sadness at every stranger's
need; else the virtuous man, incessantly dissolving like
Heraclitus in compassionate tears, nevertheless with all

this goodheartedness would become nothing but a tender-hearted idler.*

The second sort of the charitable feeling which is beautiful and amiable, indeed, but not yet the foundation of a true virtue, is *complaisance,* an inclination to be agreeable to others by friendliness, by consent to their demands, and by conformity of our conduct with their intentions. This ground of a delightful sociability is beautiful, and the pliancy of such a heart good-natured. But it is not at all a virtue, for where higher principles do not set bounds for it and weaken it, all the depravities can spring from it. For—not to mention that this complaisance toward those with whom we are concerned is very often an injustice toward others who are outside this little circle—if one takes this incitement alone, such a man can have all the depravities, not out of immediate inclination but because he likes to live so as to please others. Out of kindhearted fellowship he will be a liar, an idler, a drunkard, or the like, for he does not act by the rules that are directed to good conduct in general, but

---

* Upon a closer consideration one finds that as amiable as the compassionate quality might be, it still does not have the dignity of a virtue. A suffering child, an unfortunate though upright lady will fill our heart with this sadness, while at the same time we hear with indifference the news of a terrible battle in which, obviously, a considerable number of the human species must suffer undeservedly under horrible evil. Many a prince who has averted his face from sadness for a single unfortunate person has at the same time, and often from a vain motive, given the command to make war. Here there is no proportion in the result; how then can anyone say that the universal love of man is the cause?

rather by an inclination that in itself is beautiful but becomes trifling when it is without support and without principles.

Accordingly, true virtue can be grafted only upon principles such that the more general they are, the more sublime and noble it becomes. These principles are not speculative rules, but the consciousness of a feeling that lives in every human breast and extends itself much further than over the particular grounds of compassion and complaisance. I believe that I sum it all up when I say that it is the *feeling of the beauty and the dignity of human nature.* The first is a ground of universal affection, the second of universal esteem; and if this feeling had the greatest perfection in some one human heart, this man would of course love and prize even himself, but only so far as he is one of all those over whom his broadened and noble feeling is spread. Only when one subordinates his own inclination to one so expanded can our charitable impulses be used proportionately and bring about the noble bearing that is the beauty of virtue.

In view of the weakness of human nature and of the little force which the universal moral feeling would exercise over most hearts, Providence has placed in us as supplements to virtue assisting drives, which, as they move some of us even without principles, can also give to others who are ruled by these latter a greater thrust and a stronger impulse toward beautiful actions. Sympathy and complaisance are grounds of beautiful deeds, which would perhaps be altogether suppressed by the preponderance of a coarser selfishness; but these are not immediate grounds of virtue, as we have seen, although because they are ennobled by the relationship with it, even they gain its name. I can therefore call them *adoptive virtues*, but that which rests upon principles, *genuine virtue*. The former are beautiful and charming; the latter alone is sublime and venerable. One calls a disposition in which the first feelings rule a *kind heart*, and the man of that sort *goodhearted*; on the other hand, one rightly denotes the man who is virtuous on principle a *noble heart*, and calls him alone a *righteous* person. These adoptive virtues have, nevertheless, a great similarity to the true virtues, since they contain the feeling of an immediate pleasure in charitable and benevolent actions. The goodhearted man will go about peaceably and courteously, out of immediate complaisance without further design, and will feel sincere condolence in the misery of another.

But since even this moral sympathy is not yet enough to stimulate inert human nature to actions for the common good, Providence has placed within us still another feeling that is fine and can set us in motion or can effect a balance with coarser selfishness and common sensuality. This is the *sense of honor*, and its consequence, *shame*. The opinion others might have of our worth and their judgment of our actions is a motivation of great weight which coaxes many a sacrifice out of us. What a large part of mankind would neither have done out of an immediately arising impulse of goodheartedness, nor out of principles, happens often enough simply on account of external appearance, out of a delusion very useful although in itself very shallow—as if the judgment of others determined the worth of ourselves and our actions. What happens out of this impulse is not in the least virtuous, on account of which everyone who wants to be considered so deliberately conceals the motivation of ambition. This inclination is not even so closely related to genuine virtue as goodheartedness, because it cannot be moved immediately by the beauty of actions, but rather through their appearance of propriety when laid before strange eyes. Since nevertheless the sense of honor is a fine feeling, I can accordingly call the semblance of virtue which is motivated by it the *gloss of virtue*.

If we compare the dispositions of men, so far as one of these three kinds of feeling governs in them and determines the moral character, we shall find that each one of them stands in a closer relation with some one of the temperaments as ordinarily classified, and further that a greater deficiency of the moral feeling would be the share of the phlegmatic. Not as if the essential attribute in the character of these different temperaments depends upon the traits under consideration—for we are not concerned in this discussion with the coarser feeling, of selfishness for example, or common sensuality, and so forth, and it is of such inclinations that account is taken in the customary classification—but rather because the aforesaid finer moral feelings are apt to join more easily with one or the other of these temperaments and for the most part actually are so united.

A profound feeling for the beauty and dignity of

human nature and a firmness and determination of the mind to refer all one's actions to this as to a universal ground is earnest, and does not at all join with a changeable gaiety nor with the inconstancy of a frivolous person. It even approaches melancholy, a gentle and noble feeling so far as it is grounded upon the awe that a hard-pressed soul feels when, full of some great purpose, he sees the danger he will have to overcome, and has before his eyes the difficult but great victory of self-conquest. Thus genuine virtue based on principles has something about it which seems to harmonize most with the *melancholy* frame of mind in the moderated understanding.

Goodheartedness, a beauty and a sensitive ability of the heart to be moved with sympathy or benevolence in individual cases according to the appearance presented, is very much subject to the variation of circumstances; and as the motive of the mind does not rest upon a universal principle, it easily takes on changed forms according to whether the objects offer one or the other aspect. And as this inclination amounts to a feeling for the beautiful, it appears to unite most naturally with the temperament we call *sanguine,* which is changeable and given over to amusements. It is in this temperament that we shall have to seek the well-liked qualities we have called adoptive virtues.

The sense of honor has usually been taken as a mark of the *choleric* complexion, and the description of this character will give occasion to seek out the moral consequences of that fine feeling, which for the most part are aimed only at the gloss.

Never is a man without all traces of finer sensation; but a greater deficiency of it, a comparative apathy, occurs in the character of the *phlegmatic,* whom one deprives moreover of even the gross motives, such as lust for wealth, which nevertheless we can leave to him anyhow, together with other related inclinations, because they do not belong in this outline.

Let us now consider more closely the feelings of the sublime and beautiful, particularly so far as they are moral, under the accepted classification of the temperaments.

He whose feeling places him among the melancholy is not so named because, robbed of the joys of life, he aggrieves himself into dark dejection, but because when his feelings are aroused beyond a certain degree, or for various causes adopt a false direction, they are more easily terminated in that than in some other condition. He has above all a *feeling for the sublime.* Even beauty, for which he also has a perception, must not only delight him but move him, since it also stirs admiration in him. The enjoyment of pleasures is more earnest with him, but is none the smaller on that account. All emotions of the sublime have more fascination for him than the deceiving charms of the beautiful. His well-being will rather be satisfaction than pleasure. He is resolute. On that account he orders his sensations under principles. They are so much the less subject to inconstancy and change, the more universal this principle is to which they are subordinated, and the broader the high feeling is under which the lower are included. All particular grounds of inclination are subject to many exceptions and variations, so far as they are not derived from such a superior ground. The merry and friendly Alceste says: "I love and treasure my wife, for she is beautiful, affectionate, and clever." But how will it be when she becomes deformed by illness, and surly with age, and after the first fascination disappears seems no cleverer to you than anyone else? If the ground is no longer there, what can become of the inclination? On the other hand, let us take the kindly and steady Adraste,[3] who thinks to himself, "I will treat this person lovingly and with respect, for she is my wife." This sentiment is noble and generous. Henceforth uncertain charms may alter; she will, however, still be his wife. The noble ground remains and is not so much subject to the inconstancy of external things. Of such a nature are principles in comparison to impulses, which simply well up upon isolated occasions; and thus the man of principles is in counteraction with him who is seized opportunely by a goodhearted and loving motive. But what if the secret tongue of his heart speaks in this manner: "I must come to the aid of that man, for he suffers; not that he were perhaps my friend or companion, nor that I hold him amenable to repaying the good deed with gratitude later on. There is now no time to reason and delay with questions; he is a man, and whatever befalls men, that also concerns me." [4] Then his conduct sustains itself on the highest ground of benevolence in human nature, and is extremely sublime, because of its unchangeability as well as of the universality of its application.

I shall proceed with my observations. The man of melancholy frame of mind cares little for what others judge, what they consider good or true; he relies in this matter simply on his own insight. Because his grounds of motivation take on the nature of principles, he is not easily brought to other ideas; occasionally his steadfastness degenerates into self-will. He looks upon the change of fashions with indifference and their glitter with disdain. Friendship is sublime, and therefore belongs to his feeling. He can perhaps lose an inconstant friend; but the latter loses him not so soon. Even the remembrance of extinguished friendship is still estimable to him. Affability is beautiful, thoughtful silence sublime. He is a good guardian of his own and others' secrets. Truthfulness is sublime, and he hates lies or dissimulation. He has a high feeling of the dignity of human nature. He values himself and regards a human being as a creature who merits respect. He suffers no depraved submissiveness, and breathes freedom in a noble breast. All chains, from the gilded ones worn at court to the heavy irons of galley slaves, are abominable to him. He is a strict judge of himself and others, and not seldom is weary of himself as of the world.

In the deterioration of this character, earnestness inclines toward dejection, devotion toward fanaticism, love of freedom to enthusiasm. Insult and injustice kindle vengefulness in him. He is then much to be feared. He defies peril, and disdains death. By the perversity of his feeling and the lack of an enlightened reason he takes up the adventurous—inspirations, visions, attacks. If the

understanding is still weaker, he hits upon the grotesque
—meaningful dreams, presentiments, and miraculous
portents. He is in danger of becoming a visionary or a
crank.

He of the sanguine frame of mind has a predominating
feeling for the beautiful. Hence his joys are laughing
and lively. If he is not gay, then he is discontented, and
he little knows peaceful silence. Multiplicity is beautiful,
and he loves change. He seeks joy in himself and about
himself, amuses others, and is a good companion. He has
much moral sympathy. Others' joyfulness makes him
pleased, and their sorrow, downhearted. His moral feeling
is beautiful, but without principles, and always depends
immediately upon the impression of the moment which
objects make upon him. He is a friend of all men, or
what is to say the same thing, really never a friend although he is goodhearted and benevolent. He does not
dissemble. Today he will entertain you with his friendliness and good sorts, and tomorrow when you are ill or
in adversity he will feel true and unfeigned compassion,
but will slip gently away until the circumstances have
changed. He must never be a judge. The laws generally
seem too strict to him, and he lets himself be corrupted
by tears. He is a poor clergyman, never downright good
and never downright bad. He often yields to excess and
is wicked, more from complaisance than from inclination.
He is generous and charitable but a poor accountant of
what he owes, because he has much sensation for kindness but little for justice. No one has such a good opinion
of his own heart as he. Even if you do not esteem him,

you will still have to love him. In the greater deterioration
of his character he falls into the trifling; he is dawdling
and childish. If age does not perhaps diminish his vivacity or bestow more understanding upon him, he is in
danger of becoming an old dandy.

He whom one supposes to be of the choleric disposition has a predominant feeling for that sort of the sublime which one may call the splendid. It is actually only
the gloss of sublimity and a strong conspicuous color
which conceals the inner content of a thing or person
who perhaps is only evil and common, and deludes and
moves by appearance. Just as a building that imitates
stone carving by means of a whitewashing makes as noble
an impression as if it were really made of stone, and just
as pasted-on cornices and pilasters give the idea of solidity
although they have little hold and support nothing—in
the same way do alloyed virtues glitter, a tinsel of wisdom
and painted merit.

The choleric one considers his worth and the worth of
his possessions and actions to lie in the propriety or the
appearance with which he strikes the eye. With respect
to the inner nature and the reasons for action which the
object itself contains, he is cold, neither warmed by true
benevolence nor moved by respect.* His conduct is artful.
He must know how to take up all sorts of standpoints, in
order to appraise his own bearing from the different posi-
tions of onlookers, because he seldom asks what he is, but
only what he appears. On that account he must know

---

* He even considers himself happy only to the extent that
he supposes he is considered so by others.

well the effect upon the general taste and the various
impressions which his behavior will have on those
around him. As he has to be cold-blooded in this sly
awareness and must not let himself be blinded by love,
compassion, and sympathy, he will avoid many follies
and vexations into which a sanguine person falls, who is
fascinated by his immediate sensation. On that account
he generally appears more understanding than he really
is. His benevolence is politeness, his respect ceremony,
his love concocted flattery. He is always full of himself
when he takes up the position of a lover or a friend, and
is never either the one nor the other. He seeks to dazzle
by fashions, but because everything about him is artifi-
cial and contrived, he is stiff and awkward in them. He
behaves far more according to principles than the sanguine, who is simply moved by haphazard impressions;
but these are not principles of virtue but of reputation,
and he has no feeling for the beauty or the worth of
actions, but for the judgment that the world might pass
on them. Because his behavior, so far as one does not
look at the source from which it springs, is moreover
almost as generally useful as virtue itself, before ordinary
eyes he gains the same high esteem as the virtuous; but
before subtler eyes he conceals himself carefully, because
he well knows that the disclosure of his secret motive of
seeking repute would destroy respect for him. He is
therefore very much given to dissembling, hypocritical in
religion, a flatterer in society, and he capriciously changes
his political affiliation according to changing circumstances. He is glad to be a slave of the great, in order

thereby to be a tyrant over the petty. *Naïveté,* this noble or beautiful simplicity that bears upon itself the seal of nature and not of art, is quite foreign to him. Hence if his taste degenerates his appearance becomes *flagrant,* that is to say, swaggering in an obnoxious way. He belongs as much because of his style as of his ornamentation among the galimatias (the exaggerated), a sort of the grotesque, which is the same with respect to the splendid as the adventurous or irresponsible is with respect to the earnest sublime. In insults he falls back upon duels or lawsuits, and in civic relations upon ancestry, precedence, and title. As long as he is only vain, that is, seeks reputation and strives to catch the eye, so long can he still be tolerated; but if he becomes inflated despite an utter lack of real excellences and talents, then he is what he would least rather be considered—namely, a fool.

Since in the phlegmatic mixture no ingredients of the sublime or beautiful usually enter in any noticeable degree, this disposition does not belong in the context of our deliberations.

Of whichever sort these finer feelings might be which we have treated thus far, whether sublime or beautiful, they have the common fate that in the judgment of him who has no definite feeling in that respect, they always appear senseless and absurd. A man of a quiet and self-interested diligence has, so to speak, none of the organs with which to experience the noble bent in a poem or in a heroic virtue. He would rather read a Robinson than a Grandison,[5] and holds Cato[6] for an obstinate fool. In the same way, to persons of a somewhat earnest disposi-

tion, that seems trifling which to others is charming, and
the beguiling naïveté of a pastoral love affair to them is
insipid and childish. Furthermore, even if the mind is not
completely without a univocal finer feeling, the degrees
of its sensitivity are still very different, and we will see that
the one finds something noble and decorous which seems
to the other great but adventurous. Opportunities that
offer themselves to spy out something of the feeling of
another in nonmoral affairs can also give us occasion to
elucidate, with fair probability, his sensation with respect
to the higher mental qualities and even those of the
heart. Whoever is bored with beautiful music gives a
strong presumption that the beauties of literature and the
delicate fascinations of love will have little power over
him.

There is a certain spirit of minutiae (*esprit des baga-
telles*) which exhibits a kind of fine feeling but aims at
quite the opposite of the sublime. A taste for something
because it is very *artful* and laborious—verses that can be
read both forward and backward, riddles, clocks in finger
rings, flea chains, and so on. A taste for everything that
is overparticular and in painful fashion *orderly,* although
without use—for example, books that stand neatly ar-
rayed in long rows in bookcases, and an empty head that
looks at them and takes delight, rooms that like optical
cabinets are prim and washed extremely clean, together
with an inhospitable and morose host who inhabits them.
A taste for all that is *rare,* little though its inherent worth
otherwise might be—Epictetus' lamp, a glove of King
Charles the Twelfth; in a way, coin collecting is classed

with these. Such persons stand under great suspicion that in knowledge they will be grubs and cranks, but in morals they will be without feeling for all that is beautiful or noble in a free way.

We do an injustice to another who does not perceive the worth or the beauty of what moves or delights us, if we rejoin that *he does not understand* it. Here it does not matter so much what the *understanding* comprehends, but what the feeling senses. Nevertheless the capacities of the soul have so great a connection that for the most part one can elucidate the talents of insight from the manifestation of feeling. For it would be in vain to have bestowed these talents upon him who has many intellectual excellences, if he had not at the same time a strong feeling for the true noble or beautiful, which must be the motive to employ these gifts well and regularly.*

Now it is customary to call *useful* only what can provide a sufficiency for our coarser sensation, which can supply us a surplus in eating and drinking, display in clothing and in furniture, and lavishness in entertainment, although I do not see why everything that my most lively feeling craves should not just as well be counted

---

* One will also see that a true fineness of feeling is counted as a merit in a man. If someone can down a good dinner of meat or sweets, and then sleep incomparably well, we will indeed count it as a sign of a good digestion, but not as a merit. On the other hand, whoever can devote a part of his mealtime to listening to a piece of music or can absorb himself in a pleasant diversion with a painting, or who likes to read some witty piece even if it be only a poetical trifle, has in almost everyone's eyes the position of a more refined man, of whom one has a more favorable and laudatory opinion.

among the useful things. But everything, nevertheless, being taken on the usual terms, he whom *self-interest* governs is a man with whom one must never reason concerning the finer taste. In this respect a hen is frankly better than a parrot, a kitchen pot is more useful than a porcelain vessel, all the witty heads in the world have not the value of a peasant, and the effort to discover the distance of the fixed stars can be set aside until it has been decided how to drive the plow to best advantage. But what folly it is to let oneself into such a dispute, where it is impossible to reach a common agreement of the feelings, because feeling is by no means uniform! Nevertheless a man of the most coarse and common sensation will be able to perceive that the charms and pleasures of life which appear to be the most superfluous attract our greatest care, and that we would have few motives remaining for such abundant toils if we wanted to exclude those. Similarly, virtually no one is so gross as not to sense that a moral action, at least when done to another person, moves all the more the further it is from self-interest, and the more those nobler impulses stand out in it.

If I examine alternately the noble and the weak side of men, I reprimand myself that I am unable to take that standpoint from which these contrasts present the great portrait of the whole of human nature in a stirring form. For I willingly concede that so far as it belongs to the design of nature on the whole, these grotesque postures cannot give anything but a noble expression, although one is indeed much too shortsighted to see them in this relation. Nevertheless, in order to cast a

weak glance upon this, I believe I can set down what
follows. Among men there are but few who behave according to *principles*—which is extremely good, as it can
so easily happen that one errs in these principles, and then
the resulting disadvantage extends all the further, the
more universal the principle and the more resolute the
person who has set it before himself. Those who act
out of *goodhearted impulses* are far more numerous,
which is most excellent, although this by itself cannot
be reckoned as a particular merit of the person. Although
these virtuous instincts are sometimes lacking, on the
average they perform the great purpose of nature just
as well as those other instincts that so regularly control
the animal world. But most men are among those who
have their best-loved selves fixed before their eyes as the
only point of reference for their exertions, and who seek
to turn everything around *self-interest* as around the great
axis. Nothing can be more advantageous than this, for these
are the most diligent, orderly, and prudent; they give
support and solidity to the whole, while without intend-
ing to do so they serve the common good, provide the
necessary requirements, and supply the foundation over
which finer souls can spread beauty and harmony. Finally the *love of honor* has been disseminated to *all* men's
hearts, although in unlike measure, which must give to
the whole a beauty that is charming unto admiration. For
although ambition[7] is a foolish fancy so far as it becomes
a rule to which one subordinates the other inclinations,
nevertheless as an attendant impulse it is most admirable.
For since each one pursues actions on the great stage

according to his dominating inclinations, he is moved at the same time by a secret impulse to take a standpoint outside himself in thought, in order to judge the outward propriety of his behavior as it seems in the eyes of the onlooker. Thus the different groups unite into a picture of splendid expression, where amidst great multiplicity unity shines forth, and the whole of moral nature exhibits beauty and dignity.

Section Three

*Of the Distinction of the Beautiful and Sublime
in the Interrelations of the Two Sexes*

HE WHO FIRST CONCEIVED of woman under the name of
the *fair sex* probably wanted to say something flattering,
but he has hit upon it better than even he himself might
have believed. For without taking into consideration that
her figure in general is finer, her features more delicate
and gentler, and her mien more engaging and more
expressive of friendliness, pleasantry, and kindness than
in the male sex, and not forgetting what one must reckon
as a secret magic with which she makes our passion inclined to judgments favorable to her—even so, certain
specific traits lie especially in the personality of this sex
which distinguish it clearly from ours and chiefly result
in making her known by the mark of the beautiful. On
the other side, we could make a claim on the title of the
noble sex, if it were not required of a noble disposition
to decline honorific titles and rather to bestow than to receive them. It is not to be understood by this that woman
lacks noble qualities, or that the male sex must do without beauty completely. On the contrary, one expects that
a person of either sex brings both together, in such a
way that all the other merits of a woman should unite
solely to enhance the character of the beautiful, which

is the proper reference point; and on the other hand, among the masculine qualities the sublime clearly stands out as the criterion of his kind. All judgments of the two sexes must refer to these criteria, those that praise as well as those that blame; all education and instruction must have these before its eyes, and all efforts to advance the moral perfection of the one or the other—unless one wants to disguise the charming distinction that nature has chosen to make between the two sorts of human being. For here it is not enough to keep in mind that we are dealing with human beings; we must also remember that they are not all alike.

Women have a strong inborn feeling for all that is beautiful, elegant, and decorated. Even in childhood they like to be dressed up, and take pleasure when they are adorned. They are cleanly and very delicate in respect to all that provokes disgust. They love pleasantry and can be entertained by trivialities if only these are merry and laughing. Very early they have a modest manner about themselves, know how to give themselves a fine demeanor and be self-possessed—and this at an age when our well-bred male youth is still unruly, clumsy, and confused. They have many sympathetic sensations, goodheartedness, and compassion, prefer the beautiful to the useful, and gladly turn abundance of circumstance into parsimony, in order to support expenditure on adornment and glitter. They have very delicate feelings in regard to the least offense, and are exceedingly precise to notice the most trifling lack of attention and respect toward them. In short, they contain the chief cause in human nature for the contrast of the beautiful qualities with the noble, and they refine even the masculine sex.

I hope the reader will spare me the reckoning of the manly qualities, so far as they are parallel to the feminine, and be content only to consider both in comparison with each other. The fair sex has just as much understanding as the male, but it is a *beautiful understanding*, whereas ours should be a *deep understanding*, an expression that signifies identity with the sublime.

To the beauty of all actions belongs above all the mark that they display facility, and appear to be accomplished without painful toil. On the other hand, strivings and surmounted difficulties arouse admiration and belong to the sublime. Deep meditation and a long-sustained reflection are noble but difficult, and do not well befit a person in whom unconstrained charms should show nothing else than a beautiful nature. Laborious learning or painful pondering, even if a woman should greatly succeed in it, destroy the merits that are proper to her sex, and because of their rarity they can make of her an object of cold admiration; but at the same time they will weaken the charms with which she exercises her great power over the other sex. A woman who has a head full of Greek, like Mme Dacier,[1] or carries on fundamental controversies about mechanics, like the Marquise de Châtelet,[2] might as well even have a beard; for perhaps that would express more obviously the mien of profundity for which she strives. The beautiful understanding selects for its objects everything closely related to the finer feeling, and relinquishes to the diligent, fundamental, and deep understanding abstract speculations or branches of knowledge useful but dry. A woman therefore will learn no geometry; of the principle of sufficient reason or the monads she will know only so much as is needed to perceive the salt in a satire which the insipid grubs of our sex have censured. The fair can leave Descartes his vortices to whirl forever without troubling themselves about them, even though the suave Fontenelle[3] wished to afford them company among the planets; and the attraction of their charms loses none of its strength even if they know nothing of what Algarotti[4] has taken the trouble to sketch out for their benefit about the gravitational attraction of matter according to Newton. In history they will not fill their heads with battles, nor in geography with fortresses, for it becomes them just as little to reek of gunpowder as it does the males to reek of musk.

It appears to be a malicious stratagem of men that they have wanted to influence the fair sex to this perverted taste. For, well aware of their weakness before her natural charms and of the fact that a single sly glance sets them more in confusion than the most difficult problem of science, so soon as woman enters upon this taste they see themselves in a decided superiority and are at an advantage that otherwise they hardly would have, being able to succor their vanity in its weakness by a generous indulgence toward her. The content of woman's great science, rather, is humankind, and among humanity, men. Her philosophy is not to reason, but to sense. In the opportunity that one wants to give to women to

cultivate their beautiful nature, one must always keep
this relation before his eyes. One will seek to broaden
their total moral feeling and not their memory, and that
of course not by universal rules but by some judgment
upon the conduct that they see about them. The examples one borrows from other times in order to examine
the influence the fair sex has had in culture, the various
relations to the masculine in which it has stood in other
ages or in foreign lands, the character of both so far as it
can be illustrated by these, and the changing taste in
amusements—these comprise her whole history and geography. For the ladies, it is well to make it a pleasant
diversion to see a map setting forth the entire globe or
the principal parts of the world. This is brought about
by showing it only with the intention of portraying the
different characters of peoples that dwell there, and the
differences of their taste and moral feeling, especially in
respect to the effect these have upon the relations of the
sexes—together with a few easy illustrations taken from
the differences of their climates, or their freedom or
slavery. It is of little consequence whether or not the
women know the particular subdivisions of these lands,
their industry, power, and sovereigns. Similarly, they will
need to know nothing more of the cosmos than is necessary to make the appearance of the heavens on a beautiful evening a stimulating sight to them, if they can conceive to some extent that yet more worlds, and in them
yet more beautiful creatures, are to be found.[5] Feeling
for expressive painting and for music, not so far as it
manifests artistry but sensitivity—all this refines or ele-

vates the taste of this sex, and always has some connection with moral impulses. Never a cold and speculative instruction but always feelings, and those indeed which remain as close as possible to the situation of her sex. Such instruction is very rare because it demands talents, experience, and a heart full of feeling; and a woman can do very well without any other, as in fact without this she usually develops very well by her own efforts.

The virtue of a woman is a *beautiful virtue*.* That of the male sex should be a *noble virtue*. Women will avoid the wicked not because it is unright, but because it is ugly; and virtuous actions mean to them such as are morally beautiful. Nothing of duty, nothing of compulsion, nothing of obligation! Woman is intolerant of all commands and all morose constraint. They do something only because it pleases them, and the art consists in making only that please them which is good. I hardly believe that the fair sex is capable of principles, and I hope by that not to offend, for these are also extremely rare in the male. But in place of it Providence has put in their breast kind and benevolent sensations, a fine feeling for propriety, and a complaisant soul. One should not at all demand sacrifices and generous self-restraint. A man must never tell his wife if he risks a part of his fortune on behalf of a friend. Why should he fetter her merry talkativeness by burdening her mind with a weighty secret

---

* Above, p. [61], in a strict judgment this was called adoptive virtue; here, where on account of the character of the sex it deserves a favorable justification, it is generally called a beautiful virtue.

whose keeping lies solely upon him? Even many of her
weaknesses are, so to speak, *beautiful faults.* Offense or
misfortune moves her tender soul to sadness. A man must
never weep other than magnanimous tears. Those he
sheds in pain or over circumstances of fortune make him
contemptible. *Vanity,* for which one reproaches the fair
sex so frequently, so far as it is a fault in that sex, yet
is only a beautiful fault. For—not to mention that the
men who so gladly flatter a woman would be left in a
strait if she were not inclined to take it well—by that
they actually enliven their charms. This inclination is an
impulsion to exhibit pleasantness and good demeanor, to
let her merry wit play, to radiate through the changing
devices of dress, and to heighten her beauty. Now in
this there is not at all any offensiveness toward others,
but rather so much courtesy, if it is done with good taste,
that to scold against it with peevish rebukes is very ill-
bred. A woman who is too inconstant and deceitful is
called a coquette; which expression yet has not so harsh a
meaning as what, with a changed syllable, is applied to
man,[6] so that if we understand each other, it can sometimes indicate a familiar flattery. If vanity is a fault that
in a woman much merits excuse, a *haughty bearing* is
not only as reproachable in her as in people in general,
but completely disfigures the character of her sex. For
this quality is exceedingly stupid and ugly, and is set
completely in opposition to her captivating, modest
charms. Then such a person is in a slippery position. She
will suffer herself to be judged sharply and without any
pity; for whoever presumes an esteem invites all around

him to rebuke. Each disclosure of even the least fault gives everyone a true joy, and the word *coquette* here loses its mitigated meaning. One must always distinguish between vanity and conceit. The first seeks approbation and to some extent honors those on whose account it gives itself the trouble. The second believes itself already in full possession of approbation, and because it never strives to gain any, it wins none.

If a few ingredients of vanity do not deform a woman in the eyes of the male sex, still, the more apparent they are, the more they serve to divide the fair sex among themselves. Then they judge one another very severely, because the one seems to obscure the charms of the other, and in fact, those who make strong presumptions of conquest actually are seldom friends of one another in a true sense.

Nothing is so much set against the beautiful as disgust, just as nothing sinks deeper beneath the sublime than the ridiculous. On this account no insult can be more painful to a man than being called a *fool,* and to a woman, than being called *disgusting.* The English *Spectator* maintains that no more insulting reproach could be made to a man than if he is considered a liar, and to a woman none more bitter than if she is held unchaste.[7] I will leave this for what it is worth so far as it is judged according to strictness in morals. But here the question is not what of itself deserves the greatest rebuke, but what is actually felt as the harshest of all. And to that point I ask every reader whether, when he sets himself to thinking upon this matter, he must not assent to my opinion. The maid[8]

Ninon Lenclos[9] made not the least claims upon the
honor of chastity, and yet she would have been impla-
cably offended if one of her lovers should have gone so far
in his pronouncements; and one knows the gruesome fate
of Monaldeschi,[10] on account of an insulting expression
of that sort, at the hands of a princess who had wanted
to be thought no Lucretia.[11] It is intolerable that one
should never once be capable of doing something wicked
if one actually wanted to, because then even the omis-
sion of it remains only a very ambiguous virtue.

In order to remove ourselves as far as possible from
these disgusting things, *neatness,* which of course well
becomes any person, in the fair sex belongs among the
virtues of first rank and can hardly be pushed too high
among them, although in a man it sometimes rises to
excess and then becomes trifling.

Sensitivity to *shame* is a secrecy of nature addressed to
setting bounds to a very intractable inclination, and since
it has the voice of nature on its side, seems always to
agree with good moral qualities even if it yields to excess. Hence it is most needed, as a supplement to
principles, for there is no instance in which inclination is
so ready to turn Sophist, subtly to devise complaisant
principles, as in this. But at the same time it serves to
draw a curtain of mystery before even the most appropri-
ate and necessary purposes of nature, so that a too
familiar acquaintance with them might not occasion disgust, or indifference at least, in respect to the final purpose of an impulse onto which the finest and liveliest
inclinations of human nature are grafted. This quality is

especially peculiar to the fair sex and very becoming to it.
There is also a coarse and contemptible rudeness in put-
ting delicate modesty to embarrassment or annoyance by
the sort of vulgar jests called obscenities. However,
although one may go as far around the secret as one ever
will, the sexual inclination still ultimately underlies all
her remaining charms, and a woman, ever as a woman, is
the pleasant object of a well-mannered conversation; and
this might perhaps explain why otherwise polite men occasionally take the liberty to let certain fine allusions show
through, by a little mischief in their jests, which make us
call them *loose* or *waggish*. Because they neither affront
by searching glances nor intend to injure anyone's
esteem, they believe it justified to call the person who
receives it with an indignant or brittle mien a *prude*. I
mention this practice only because it is generally considered as a somewhat bold trait in polite conversation,
and also because in point of fact much wit has been
squandered upon it; however, judgment according to
moral strictness does not belong here, because what I have
to observe and explain in the sensing of the beautiful is
only the appearances.

The noble qualities of this sex, which still, as we have
already noted, must never disguise the feeling of the
beautiful, proclaim themselves by nothing more clearly
and surely than by *modesty*, a sort of noble simplicity
and innocence in great excellences. Out of it shines a
quiet benevolence and respect toward others, linked at
the same time with a certain *noble trust* in oneself, and
a reasonable self-esteem that is always to be found in a

sublime disposition. Since this fine mixture at once captivates by charms and moves by respect, it puts all the remaining shining qualities in security against the mischief of censure and mockery. Persons of this temperament also have a heart for friendship, which in a woman can never be valued highly enough, because it is so rare and moreover must be so exceedingly charming.

As it is our purpose to judge concerning feelings, it cannot be unpleasant to bring under concepts, if possible, the difference of the impression that the form and features of the fair sex make on the masculine. This complete fascination is really overlaid upon the sex instinct. Nature pursues its great purpose, and all refinements that join together, though they may appear to stand as far from that as they will, are only trimmings and borrow their charm ultimately from that very source. A healthy and *coarse taste,* which always stays very close to this impulse, is little tempted by the charms of demeanor, of facial features, of eyes, and so on, in a woman, and because it really pertains only to sex, it oftentimes sees the delicacy of others as empty flirting.

If this taste is not fine, nevertheless it is not on that account to be disdained. For the largest part of mankind complies by means of it with the great order of nature, in a very simple and sure way.* Through it the greatest

---

* As all things in the world have their bad side, regarding this taste it is only to be regretted that easier than another it degenerates into dissoluteness. For as any other can extinguish the fire one person has lighted, there are not enough obstacles that can confine an intractable inclination.

number of marriages are brought about, and indeed by
the most diligent part of the human race; and because
the man does not have his head full of fascinating expressions, languishing eyes, noble demeanor, and so forth,
and understands nothing of all this, he becomes that
much the more attentive to householders' virtues, thrift
and such, and to the dowry. As for what relates to the
somewhat finer taste, on whose account it might be necessary to make a distinction among the exterior charms of
women, this is fixed either upon what in the form and
the expression of the face is moral, or upon what is nonmoral. In respect to the last-named sort of pleasantness,
a lady is called *pretty*. A well-proportioned figure, regular
features, colors of eyes and face which contrast prettily,
beauties pure and simple which are also pleasing in a
bouquet and gain a cool approbation. The face itself
says nothing, although it is pretty, and speaks not to the
heart. What is moral in the expression of the features,
the eyes, and mien pertains to the feeling either of the
sublime or of the beautiful. A woman in whom the
agreeableness beseeming her sex particularly makes mani-
fest the moral expression of the sublime is called *beautiful* in the proper sense; so far as the moral composition
makes itself discernible in the mien or facial features,
she whose features show qualities of beauty is *agreeable*,
and if she is that to a high degree, *charming*. The first,
under a mien of composure and a noble demeanor, lets
the glimmer of a beautiful understanding play forth
through discreet glances, and as in her face she portrays
a tender feeling and a benevolent heart, she seizes pos-

session of the affection as well as the esteem of a masculine heart. The second exhibits merriment and wit in laughing eyes, something of fine mischief, the playfulness of jest and sly coyness. She charms, while the first moves; and the feeling of love of which she is capable and which she stimulates in others is fickle but beautiful, whereas the feeling of the first is tender, combined with respect, and constant. I do not want to engage in too detailed an analysis of this sort, for in doing so the author always appears to depict his own inclination. I shall still mention, however, that the liking many women have for a healthy but pale color can be explained here. For this generally accompanies a disposition of more inward feeling and delicate sensation, which belongs to the quality of the sublime; whereas the rosy and blooming complexion proclaims less of the first, but more of the joyful and merry disposition—but it is more suitable to vanity to move and to arrest, than to charm and to attract. On the other hand there can be very pretty persons completely without moral feeling and without any expression that indicates feeling; but they will neither move nor charm, unless it might be the coarse taste of which we have made mention, which sometimes grows somewhat more refined and then also selects after its fashion. It is too bad that this sort of beautiful creatures easily fall into the fault of *conceit,* through the consciousness of the beautiful figure their mirror shows them, and from a lack of finer sensations, for then they make all indifferent to them except the flatterer, who has ulterior motives and contrives intrigues.

Perhaps by following these concepts one can understand something of the different effect the figure of the
same woman has upon the tastes of men. I do not concern
myself with what in this impression relates too closely to
the sex impulse and may be of a piece with the particular
sensual illusion with which the feeling of everyone
clothes itself, because it lies outside the compass of finer
taste. Perhaps what M. Buffon supposes may be true:
that the figure that makes the first impression, at the time
when this impulse is still new and is beginning to develop, remains the pattern all feminine figures in the
future must more or less follow so as to be able to stir
the fanciful ardor, whereby a rather coarse inclination is
compelled to choose among the different objects of a
sex.[12] Regarding the somewhat finer taste, I affirm that
the sort of beauty we have called the *pretty figure* is
judged by all men very much alike, and that opinions
about it are not so different as one generally maintains.
The Circassian and Georgian maidens have always been
considered extremely pretty by all Europeans who travel
through their lands. The Turks, the Arabs, the Persians
are apparently of one mind in this taste, because they
are very eager to beautify their races through such fine
blood, and one also notes that the Persian race has actually
succeeded in this. The merchants of Hindustan likewise
do not fail to draw great profit from a wicked commerce
in such beautiful creatures, for they supply them to the
self-indulgent rich men of their land. And it appears
that, as greatly as the caprice of taste in these different
quarters of the world may diverge, still, whatever is once

known in any of these as especially pretty will also be
considered the same in all the others. But whenever what
is moral in the features mingles in the judgment upon the
fine figure, the taste of different men is always very different, both because their moral feeling itself is dissimilar, and also on account of the different meaning
that the expression of the face may have in every fancy.
One finds that those formations that at first glance do not
have any particular effect, because they are not pretty in
any decided way, generally appear far more to captivate
and to grow constantly more beautiful as soon as they
begin to please upon nearer acquaintance. On the other
hand, the pretty appearance that proclaims itself at once
is later received with greater indifference. This probably
is because moral charms, when they are evident, are all
the more arresting because they are set in operation only
on the occasion of moral sensations, and let themselves
be discovered in this way, each disclosure of a new charm
causing one to suspect still more of these; whereas all the
agreeable features that do not at all conceal themselves,
after exercising their entire effect at the beginning, can
subsequently do nothing more than to cool off the enamored curiosity and bring it gradually to indifference.

Along with these observations, the following comment
naturally presents itself. The quite simple and coarse
feeling in the sexual inclination leads directly to the
great purpose of nature, and as it fulfills her claims it is
fitted to make the person himself happy without digres-
sion; but because of its great universality it degenerates
easily into excess and dissoluteness. On the other hand,

a very refined taste serves to take away the wildness of an impetuous inclination, and although it limits this to few objects, to make it modest and decorous, such an inclination usually misses the great goal of nature. As it demands or expects more than nature usually offers, it seldom takes care to make the person of such delicate feeling happy. The first disposition becomes uncouth, because it is attracted to all the members of a sex; the second becomes oversubtle, because actually it is attracted to none. It is occupied only with an object that the enamored inclination creates in thought, and ornaments with all the noble and beautiful qualities that nature seldom unites in one human being and still more seldom brings to him who can value them and perhaps would be worthy of such a possession. Thence arises the postponement and finally the full abandonment of the marital bond; or what is perhaps just as bad, a peevish regret after making a choice that does not fulfill the great expectations one had made oneself—for not seldom the Aesopian cock finds a pearl when a common barleycorn would have been better suited to him.

From this we can perceive in general that as charming as the impressions of the delicate feeling may be, one still might have cause to be on guard in its refinement, lest by excessive sensibility we subtly fabricate only much discontent and a source of evil. To noble souls I might well propose to refine as much as they can the feeling with respect to qualities that become them, or with respect to actions that they themselves perform, but to maintain this taste in its simplicity respecting what they enjoy or

expect from others—if only I saw how this were possible
to achieve. But if it were approached, they would make
others happy and also be happy themselves. It is never
to be lost sight of that in whatever way it might be, one
must make no very high claims upon the raptures of life
and the perfection of men; for he who always expects
only something ordinary has the advantage that the
result seldom refutes his hope, but sometimes he is sur-
prised by quite unexpected perfections.

Finally age, the great destroyer of beauty, threatens
all these charms; and if it proceeds according to the
natural order of things, gradually the sublime and noble
qualities must take the place of the beautiful, in order
to make a person always worthy of a greater respect as
she ceases to be attractive. In my opinion, the whole perfection of the fair sex in the bloom of years should con-
sist in the beautiful simplicity that has been brought to
its height by a refined feeling toward all that is charming
and noble. Gradually, as the claims upon charms diminish, the reading of books and the broadening of insight
could refill unnoticed the vacant place of the Graces
with the Muses, and the husband should be the first
instructor. Nevertheless, when the epoch of growing old,
so terrible to every woman, actually approaches, she still
belongs to the fair sex, and that sex disfigures itself if in
a kind of despair of holding this character longer, it
gives way to a surly and irritable mood.

An aged person who attends a gathering with a modest
and friendly manner, is sociable in a merry and sensible
way, favors with a pleasant demeanor the pleasures of

youth in which she herself no longer participates, and, as she looks after everything, manifests contentment and benevolence toward the joys that are going on around her, is yet a finer person that a man of like age and perhaps even more attractive than a girl, although in another sense. Indeed the platonic love might well be somewhat too mystical, which an ancient philosopher asserted when he said of the object of his inclination, "The Graces reside in her wrinkles, and my soul seems to hover upon my lips when I kiss her withered mouth"; but such claims must then be relinquished. An old man who acts infatuated is a fool, and the like presumptions of the other sex at that age are disgusting. It never is due to nature when we do not appear with a good demeanor, but rather to the fact that we turn her upside down.

In order to keep close to my text, I want to undertake a few reflections on the influence one sex can have upon the other, to beautify or ennoble its feeling. Woman has a superior feeling for the beautiful, so far as it pertains to herself; but for the noble, so far as it is encountered in the male sex. Man on the other hand has a decided feeling for the noble, which belongs to his qualities, but for the beautiful, so far as it is to be found in woman. From this it must follow that the purposes of nature are directed still more to ennoble man, by the sexual inclination, and likewise still more to beautify woman. A woman is embarrassed little that she does not possess certain high insights, that she is timid, and not fit for serious employments, and so forth; she is beautiful and captivates, and that is enough. On the other hand, she demands all these qualities in a man, and the sublimity of her soul shows itself only in that she knows to treasure these noble qualities so far as they are found in him. How else indeed would it be possible that so many grotesque male faces, whatever merits they may possess, could gain such well-bred and fine wives! Man on the other hand is much more delicate in respect to the beautiful charms of woman. By their fine figure, merry naïveté, and charming friendliness he is sufficiently repaid for the lack of book learning and for other deficiencies that he must supply by his own talents. Vanity and fashion can give these natural drives a false direction and make out of many a male a *sweet gentleman,* but out of a woman either a prude or an Amazon; but still nature always seeks to reassert her own order. One can thereby judge what powerful influences the sexual inclination could have especially upon the male sex, to ennoble it, if instead of many dry instructions the moral feeling of woman were seasonably developed to sense properly what belongs to the dignity and the sublime qualities of the other sex, and were thus prepared to look upon the trifling fops with disdain and to yield to no other qualities than the merits. It is also certain that the power of her charms on the whole would gain through that; for it is apparent that their fascination for the most part works only upon nobler souls; the others are not fine enough to sense them. Just as the poet Simonides said, when someone advised him to let the Thessalians hear his beautiful songs: "These fellows are too stupid to be beguiled by such a man as I am." It has been regarded moreover as an effect of association with the fair sex that men's customs have become gentler, their conduct more polite and refined, and their bearing more elegant; but the advantage of this is only incidental.* The principal object is that the man should become more perfect as a man, and the woman as a wife; that is, that the motives of the sexual inclination work according to the hint of nature, still more to ennoble the one and to beautify the qualities of the other. If all comes to the extreme, the man, confident in his merits, will be able to say: "Even if you do not love me, I will constrain you to esteem me," and the woman, secure in the might of her charms, will answer: "Even if you do not inwardly admire me, I will still constrain you to love me." In default of such principles one sees men take on femininity in order to please, and woman occasionally (although much more seldom) affect a masculine demeanor in order to stimulate esteem; but whatever one does contrary to nature's will, one always does very poorly.

In matrimonial life the united pair should, as it were, constitute a single moral person, which is animated and governed by the understanding of the man and the taste of the wife. For not only can one credit more insight

---

* This advantage itself is really much reduced by the observation that one will have made, that men who are too early and too frequently introduced into company where woman sets the tone generally become somewhat trifling, and in male society they are boring or even contemptible because they have lost the taste for conversation, which must be merry, to be sure, but still of actual content—witty, to be sure, but also useful through its earnest discourse.

founded on experience to the former, and more freedom and accuracy in sensation to the latter; but also, the more sublime a disposition is, the more inclined it is to place the greatest purpose of its exertions in the contentment of a beloved object, and likewise the more beautiful it is, the more it seeks to requite these exertions by complaisance. In such a relation, then, a dispute over precedence is trifling and, where it occurs, is the surest sign of a coarse or dissimilarly matched taste. If it comes to such a state that the question is of the right of the superior to command, then the case is already utterly corrupted; for where the whole union is in reality erected solely upon inclination, it is already half destroyed as soon as the "duty" begins to make itself heard. The presumption of the woman in this harsh tone is extremely ugly, and of the man is base and contemptible in the highest degree. However, the wise order of things so brings it about that all these niceties and delicacies of feeling have their whole strength only in the beginning, but subsequently gradually become duller through association and domestic concerns, and then degenerate into familiar love. Finally, the great skill consists in still preserving sufficient remainders of those feelings so that indifference and satiety do not put an end to the whole value of the enjoyment on whose account it has solely and alone been worth the trouble to enter such a union.

Of National Characteristics, so far as They
Depend upon the Distinct Feeling of the
Beautiful and Sublime*

OF THE PEOPLES OF OUR PART of the world, in my
opinion those who distinguish themselves among all
others by the feeling for the beautiful are the Italians
and the French, but by the feeling for the sublime, the
Germans, English, and Spanish. Holland can be considered as that land where the finer taste becomes largely
unnoticeable. The beautiful itself is either fascinating
and moving, or laughing and delightful. The first has
something of the sublime in it, and the mind in this
feeling is thoughtful and enraptured, but in the second

---

* My intention is not at all to portray the characters of
peoples in detail, but I sketch only a few features that express
the feeling of the sublime and the beautiful which they show.
One can readily imagine that in such a picture only a passing
justice could be demanded, that its prototypes stand out only in
the great multitude of those who lay claim to a finer feeling, and
that no nation lacks dispositions that combine the most excellent
qualities of this sort. On that account the blame that might occasionally fall upon a people can offend no one, for it is of such a
nature that each one can hit it like a ball to his neighbor.
Whether these national differences are contingent and depend
upon the times and the type of government, or are bound by a
certain necessity to the climate, I do not here inquire.

sort of feeling, smiling and joyful. The first sort of beautiful feeling seems to be excellently suited to the Italians,
and the second, to the French. In the national character
that bears the expression of the sublime, this is either
that of the terrifying sort, which is a little inclined to the
adventurous, or it is a feeling for the noble, or for the
splendid. I believe I have reason to be able to ascribe
the feeling of the first sort to the Spaniard, the second
to the Englishman, and the third to the German. The
feeling for the splendid is not original by nature, like
the remaining kinds of taste; and although a spirit of
imitation can be united with every other feeling, it
really is more peculiar to the glittering sublime; for this
is properly a mixed feeling combining the beautiful and
the sublime, in which each taken by itself is colder, so
that the mind is free enough by means of their combination to attend to examples, and in fact it stands in need
of the impulsion of such examples. Accordingly, the
German will have less feeling in respect to the beautiful
than the Frenchman, and less of what pertains to the
sublime than the Englishman; but instances in which both
appear in combination will be more suitable to his feeling, as he will fortunately escape the faults into which
an excessive strength of either of these sorts of feeling
could fall.

I shall mention only fleetingly the arts and the sciences,
the choice of which can confirm the taste of the nations
which we have imputed to them. The Italian genius has
distinguished itself especially in music, painting, sculp-

ture, and architecture. All these beautiful arts encounter a similarly fine taste in France, although their beauty there is less moving. Taste in respect to poetic or oratorical perfection in France falls more into the beautiful, in England more into the sublime. Fine jests, comedy, laughing satire, enamored flirting, and light and naturally flowing writing are native to France. In England, on the other hand, are thoughts of profound content, tragedy, the epic poem, and in general the solid gold of wit, which under French hammers can be stretched to thin leaves of great surface. In Germany wit still shines very much through a foil. Earlier, it was flagrant, but through examples and by the understanding of the nation it has become more charming and noble—but the first with less naïveté, the second with a less bold energy, than in the aforementioned peoples. The taste of the Dutch nation for a painful order and a grace that stirs one to solicitude and embarrassment causes one to expect little feeling also in regard to the inartificial and free movements of the genius, whose beauty would only be deformed by the anxious prevention of faults. Nothing can be more set against all art and science than an adventurous taste, because this distorts nature, which is the archetype of all the beautiful and noble. Hence the Spanish nation has displayed little feeling for the beautiful arts and sciences.

The mental characters of peoples are most discernible by whatever in them is moral, on which account we will yet take under consideration their different feelings in

respect to the sublime and beautiful from this point of
view.*

The Spaniard is earnest, taciturn, and truthful. There
are few more honest merchants in the world than the
Spanish.[1] He has a proud soul and more feeling for great
than for beautiful actions. In his composition little of the
kind and gentle benevolence is to be encountered; thus
he is often harsh and indeed quite cruel. The auto da
fé is maintained not so much by superstition as by the
adventurous inclination of the nation, aroused by the
pomp and terror of a rite in which one sees the *San
Benito,* daubed with diabolic figures,[2] committed to the
flames kindled in an access of devotion. One cannot say
that the Spaniard is haughtier or more amorous than anyone of another people; but he is both in an adventurous
way, which is odd and exceptional. Letting the plow
stand and walking with long sword and mantle up and
down the tilled fields until the traveling stranger has
passed; or in a bullfight, where for once the beautiful of
the land are seen unveiled, to proclaim his ladylove by a
special salute and then to risk his life in her honor in a
dangerous battle with a wild beast—these are exceptional
and odd actions, which deviate far from the natural.

The Italian appears to have a feeling mixed from that
of a Spaniard and that of a Frenchman, more feeling for

* It is hardly necessary that I repeat here my foregoing
apology. In each folk the finest part contains praiseworthy characters of all kinds, and whoever is affected by one or another reproach will, if he is fine enough, understand the advantage that
follows when he relinquishes all the others to their fate but
makes an exception of himself.

the beautiful than the former and more for the sublime
than the latter. In this way, as I think, the remaining
traits of his moral character can be explained.

The Frenchman has a predominant feeling for the
morally beautiful. He is gracious, courteous, and complaisant. He becomes familiar very quickly, is jesting and
free in society, and the expression "a *man* or a *lady of
good tone*" has an understandable meaning only for him
who has acquired the polite feeling of a Frenchman. Even
his sublime sensations, of which he has not a few, are
subordinated to the feeling of the beautiful and obtain
their strength only through harmony with the latter. He
likes very much to be witty and will without hesitation
sacrifice something of the truth for a conceit. On the
other hand, where one cannot be witty,* he displays just
as profound an insight as someone from any other country, for example in mathematics and in the other dry or
profound arts and sciences. To him a *bon mot* has not a
fleeting worth, as elsewhere; it is eagerly spread about
and preserved in books like the most momentous event.
He is a quiet citizen and revenges himself against the
oppressions of the farmers-general by satires, or by re-
monstrances in parliament, which, when they have
given the fathers of the people a beautiful patriotic as-

---

* In metaphysics, ethics, and theology, one cannot be cautious enough of the publications of this nation. Commonly there
prevails in them much beautiful delusion, which in a cold inquiry does not hold up under the test. The Frenchman loves the
bold in his declarations; but in order to attain the truth, one must
be not bold but cautious. In history he loves anecdotes, to which
nothing more is lacking than to wish that only they were true.

pect as intended, do nothing further than to become
crowned by a glorious rebuke, and are celebrated in
ingenious elegies. The object to which the merits and
national talents of this people refer most often is woman.*
Not as if she were loved or treasured here more than
elsewhere, but because she gives the best occasion to
display in her light the most favorite talents of wit,
politeness, and good manners. Besides, a vain person of
either sex always loves only himself; to him, the opposite
sex is merely a plaything. The Frenchman does not actually lack noble qualities, but these can be brought to life
only by the feeling of the beautiful; thus the fair sex
here would be able to have a mightier influence to arouse
the noblest deeds of the male and to set them astir than
perhaps anywhere else in the world, if one were minded

---

* In France, woman gives the tone to all companies and all
society. Now of course it cannot be denied that gatherings without the fair sex are rather tasteless and boring; but if the lady
gives the beautiful tone, so should the man on his side give the
noble. Failing that, the society becomes just as boring, but from
an opposite reason, for nothing disgusts so much as excessive
sweetness. In the French taste it is not worded, "Is the gentleman
at home?" but "Is Madame at home?" "Madame is at her toilette,"
"Madame has vapors" (a sort of beautiful caprice); in short, with
Madame and by Madame are all conversations and all pleasures
kept occupied. However, the woman is not at all more honored
by this. A man who flirts is always without feeling, as well of
true respect as of tender love. I would certainly not have wanted
to say what Rousseau so boldly asserts, that a woman never becomes anything more than a grown-up child. But the sharpsighted
Swiss wrote this in France and presumably, as such a great
defender of the fair sex, he felt indignation that it is not treated
there with more real respect.

to favor this bent of the national spirit a little. It is a pity that the lilies do not spin.

The fault on which this national character borders nearest is the trifling, or with a more polite expression, the frivolous. Weighty matters are treated as sport, and trivialities serve for the most earnest business. In old age the Frenchman still sings sportive songs, and is, as much as he can be, still gallant toward the ladies. In these remarks I have great authorities from this nation itself on my side, and I retreat behind a Montesquieu or a D'Alembert, in order to be safe against any anxious indignation.

The Englishman is cool in the beginning of every acquaintance, and indifferent toward a stranger. He has little inclination to small complaisances; on the other hand, as soon as he is a friend, he is laid under great performances of service. He takes little trouble to be witty in society, or to display a polite demeanor; but rather, he is reasonable and steady. He is a bad imitator, cares very little about what others judge, and follows solely his own taste. In relation to woman he is not of French politeness,

_____

[Rousseau in *Emile* says "Les mâles, en qui l'on empêche le développement ultérieur du sexe, gardent cette conformité toute leur vie; ils sont toujours de grands enfants: et les femmes, ne perdant point cette même conformité, semblent, à bien des égards, ne jamais être autre chose." Kant has apparently taken the phrase modifying "femmes" as nonrestrictive. Rousseau's English translator makes it restrictive: ". . . women who never lose this resemblance seem in many respects never to be more than children." The latter better fits the context. (Jean-Jacques Rousseau, *Emile ou de l'Education,* ed. Ernest Flammarion [Paris, n.d.], p. 272; and *Emile,* tr. Barbara Foxley [London, 1911], p. 172.)]

but displays toward her far more respect, and perhaps carries this too far, as in marriage he generally grants to his wife an unlimited esteem. He is steadfast, sometimes to the point of obstinacy, bold and determined, often to audacity, and acts according to principles generally to the point of being headstrong. He easily becomes an eccentric, not out of vanity but because he concerns himself little about others, and does not easily do violence to his taste out of complaisance or imitation; on that account he is seldom as much loved as the Frenchman, but when he is well known, generally more highly esteemed.

The German has a feeling mixed from that of an Englishman and that of a Frenchman, but appears to come nearer to the first, and any greater similarity to the latter is only affected and imitated. He has a fortunate combination of feeling, both in that of the sublime and in that of the beautiful; and if in the first he does not equal an Englishman, nor in the second a Frenchman, he yet surpasses both so far as he unites them. He displays more complaisance in society than the first, and if indeed he does not bring as much pleasant liveliness and wit into the company as the Frenchman, still he expresses more moderation and understanding. In love, just as in all forms of taste, he is reasonably methodical, and because he combines the beautiful with the noble he is cool enough in each feeling to occupy his mind with reflections upon demeanor, splendor, and appearances. Therefore family, title, and rank, in civil relations as well as in love, are of great significance to him. Far more than the aforementioned nationalities, he asks *how people might judge him;* and if there is something in his character which could arouse the wish for a general improvement, it is this weakness whereby he does not venture to be original although he has all the talents needed for that, and occupies himself too much with the opinion of others. This takes away all support from his moral qualities, as it makes them fickle and falsely contrived.

The Dutchman is of an orderly and diligent disposition and, as he looks solely to the useful, he has little feeling for what in the finer understanding is beautiful or sublime. A great man signifies exactly the same to him as a rich man, by a friend he means his correspondent, and a visit that makes him no profit is very boring to him. He contrasts as much with a Frenchman as with an Englishman, and in a way he is a German become very phlegmatic.

If we apply the inquiry into these ideas in a given instance, for example, the sense of honor, the following national differences are exhibited. The feeling for honor in the Frenchman is *vanity,* in the Spaniard *haughtiness,* in the Englishman *pride,* in the German *pomp,* and in the Dutchman *conceit.* These expressions appear at first glance to mean the same thing, but in the richness of our German language they denote very discernible distinctions. *Vanity* strives for approbation, is fickle and changeable, but its outward behavior is *courteous.* The *haughty* one is full of falsely fancied great merits and seeks very little to obtain the approval of others; his conduct is stiff and *bombastic. Pride* is really only a greater consciousness of one's own worth, which often can be very correct (on which account it is also occasionally called a noble pride; but I can never speak of a noble haughtiness, because this always indicates an incorrect and exaggerated estimation of oneself); the behavior of the proud toward others is *indifferent* and cold. The *pompous* person is a proud one who at the same time is vain.* But the approval he seeks from others consists in merely the marks of respect. Hence he likes to glitter through title, ancestry, and pageantry. The German is especially infected by this weakness. The words gracious, most gracious, highborn, and wellborn, and more such bombast, make his language stiff and awkward, and indeed very much hinder the beautiful simplicity other people can give to their style. The behavior of a pompous person in society is *ceremony*. The *conceited* is a haughty person who shows clear signs of the contempt of others in his behavior. In his conduct he is *rude*. This wretched quality deviates most from finer taste, because it is obviously stupid; for it is certainly not the means to satisfy the sense of honor, by open contempt to challenge all around him to hatred and to biting mockery.

In love the Germans and the English have rather healthy inclinations, a bit delicate in feeling but rather more of a hale and hearty taste. In this point the Italian is sophistical, the Spaniard visionary, the Frenchman dainty.

---

* It is not necessary that a pompous one be haughty also, that is to say, to make himself an exaggerated, false fancy of his merits; it could be, perhaps, that he does not value himself more highly than he deserves, but only has a false taste in making his worth show to advantage externally.

The religion of our part of the world is not a matter of an arbitrary taste, but is of a more estimable origin. Therefore only the excesses in it and what appertains exclusively to man give indications of the different national qualities. I bring these excesses under the following headings: *credulity, superstition, fanaticism,* and *indifferentism.*[3] The *credulous* is for the most part the ignorant portion of every nation, which, however, has no perceptible finer feeling. Persuasion depends solely on hearsay and the appearance of authority, without any sort of finer feeling containing the motive to it. For examples of whole peoples of this sort, one must seek in the north. The credulous person, if he is of adventurous taste, becomes *superstitious.* This taste is in itself a ground to believe something more easily,* and of two men of whom the one is infected with the feeling but the other is of cool and moderate disposition, the first, even if he really has more understanding, will nevertheless be led astray by his dominating inclination to believe something unnatural sooner than the other, who is protected from this exaggeration not by his insight but by his common phlegmatic feeling. The superstitious one in religion likes to place

---

* One has observed besides that the English, although a very clever people, can be easily ensnared by a confident announcement of a strange and absurd thing into believing it at first—whereof one has many examples. But a bold disposition, prepared by different experiences in which so many strange things nevertheless were found true, breaks quickly through those little scruples by which a weak and mistrustful head is soon detained and thus guarded occasionally from error without earning that result.

between himself and the highest object of reverence certain mighty and astonishing men, giants so to speak of holiness, whom nature obeys and whose adjuring voices open or close the iron gates of Tartarus, who have their feet still standing on the earth beneath while they touch Heaven with their heads. In Spain, accordingly, the instruction of sound reason will have great obstacles to overcome, not because it has to drive out ignorance but because an odd taste confronts it, to which the natural is mean, and which never believes itself to be in a sublime feeling if its object is not adventurous. *Fanaticism* is, so to speak, a pious arrogance, and is induced by a certain pride and a quite too great self-confidence to get nearer to heavenly natures and to elevate itself by an astonishing flight over the usual and prescribed order. The fanatic speaks only of immediate inspiration and of the meditative life, whereas the superstitious one makes vows before the pictures of great wonder-working saints and places his trust in the fancied and inimitable excellences of other persons of his own nature. Even the excesses, as we have remarked above, bear indications of the national feeling, and thus fanaticism,* at least in times past, was most to be found in Germany and England, and

---

* Fanaticism must always be distinguished from *enthusiasm*. The former believes itself to feel an immediate and extraordinary communion with a higher nature; the latter means the state of the mind in which it has become inflamed by any principle above the proper degree, whether it might be by maxims of patriotic virtue, or of friendship, or of religion, without the illusion of a supernatural communion having anything to do with it.

is, so to speak, an unnatural outgrowth of the noble feeling that belongs to the character of these peoples. It is on the whole far less pernicious than the superstitious inclination even though it is violent at the outset, because the inflammation of a fanatical spirit gradually cools and by its nature must finally reach an orderly moderation, whereas superstition unnoticed takes deeper root in a quiet and passive constitution and completely takes away from the enchained man the confidence ever to free himself from a pernicious delusion. Finally, a vain and frivolous person is always without stronger feeling for the sublime, and his religion is without emotion, for the most part only a thing of fashion, which he attends with all politeness while remaining cold. This is the practical *indifferentism* to which the French national spirit appears to be the most inclined, from which it is only a step to sacrilegious mockery and which, when one looks at its inner worth, basically has little superiority over a complete abnegation.

If we cast a fleeting glance over the other parts of the world, we find the Arab the noblest man in the Orient, yet of a feeling that degenerates very much into the adventurous. He is hospitable, generous, and truthful; yet his narrative and history and on the whole his feeling are always interwoven with some wonderful thing. His inflamed imagination presents things to him in unnatural and distorted images, and even the propagation of his religion was a great adventure. If the Arabs are, so to speak, the Spaniards of the Orient, similarly the Persians are the French of Asia. They are good poets, courteous

and of fairly fine taste. They are not such strict followers
of Islam, and they permit to their pleasure-prone disposition a tolerably mild interpretation of the Koran. The
Japanese could in a way be regarded as the Englishmen
of this part of the world, but hardly in any other quality
than their resoluteness—which degenerates into the utmost stubbornness—their valor, and disdain of death. For
the rest, they display few signs of a finer feeling. The
Indians have a dominating taste of the grotesque, of the
sort that falls into the adventurous. Their religion consists of grotesqueries. Idols of monstrous form, the price-
less tooth of the mighty monkey Hanuman, the unnatural atonements of the fakirs (heathen mendicant
friars) and so forth are in this taste. The despotic sacrifice of wives in the very same funeral pyre that consumes
the corpse of the husband is a hideous excess. What
trifling grotesqueries do the verbose and studied compliments of the Chinese contain! Even their paintings are
grotesque and portray strange and unnatural figures such
as are encountered nowhere in the world. They also have
venerable grotesqueries because they are of very ancient
custom,* and no nation in the world has more of these
than this one.

The Negroes of Africa have by nature no feeling that
rises above the trifling. Mr. Hume challenges anyone

---

* In Pekin they still carry on the ceremony, in an eclipse
of the sun or moon, of driving away with a great noise the
dragon that wants to devour these heavenly bodies; and thus they
preserve a miserable custom from the most ancient times of
ignorance, although they are now so much better informed.

to cite a single example in which a Negro has shown
talents, and asserts that among the hundreds of thousands
of blacks who are transported elsewhere from their
countries, although many of them have even been set
free, still not a single one was ever found who presented
anything great in art or science or any other praiseworthy quality, even though among the whites some
continually rise aloft from the lowest rabble, and through
superior gifts earn respect in the world.[4] So fundamental
is the difference between these two races of man, and
it appears to be as great in regard to mental capacities as
in color. The religion of fetishes so widespread among
them is perhaps a sort of idolatry that sinks as deeply into
the trifling as appears to be possible to human nature.
A bird feather, a cow's horn, a conch shell, or any other
common object, as soon as it becomes consecrated by a
few words, is an object of veneration and of invocation in
swearing oaths. The blacks are very vain but in the
Negro's way, and so talkative that they must be driven
apart from each other with thrashings.

Among all savages there is no nation that displays so
sublime a mental character as those of North America.
They have a strong feeling for honor, and as in quest of
it they seek wild adventures hundreds of miles abroad,
they are still extremely careful to avert the least injury
to it when their equally harsh enemy, upon capturing
them, seeks by cruel pain to extort cowardly groans from
them. The Canadian savage, moreover, is truthful and
honest. The friendship he establishes is just as adventurous and enthusiastic as anything of that kind reported

from the most ancient and fabled times. He is extremely proud, feels the whole worth of freedom, and even in his education suffers no encounter that would let him feel a low subservience. Lycurgus probably gave statutes to just such savages; and if a lawgiver arose among the Six Nations, one would see a Spartan republic rise in the New World; for the undertaking of the Argonauts is little different from the war parties of these Indians, and Jason excels Attakakullakulla[5] in nothing but the honor of a Greek name. All these savages have little feeling for the beautiful in moral understanding, and the generous forgiveness of an injury, which is at once noble and beautiful, is completely unknown as a virtue among the savages, but rather is disdained as a miserable cowardice. Valor is the greatest merit of the savage and revenge his sweetest bliss. The remaining natives of this part of the world show few traces of a mental character disposed to the finer feelings, and an extraordinary apathy constitutes the mark of this type of race.

If we examine the relation of the sexes in these parts of the world, we find that the European alone has found the secret of decorating with so many flowers the sensual charm of a mighty inclination and of interlacing it with so much morality that he has not only extremely elevated its agreeableness but has also made it very decorous. The inhabitant of the Orient is of a very false taste in this respect. Since he has no concept of the morally beautiful which can be united with this impulse, he loses even the worth of the sensuous enjoyment, and his harem is a

constant source of unrest. He thrives on all sorts of
amorous grotesqueries, among which the imaginary jewel
is only the foremost, which he seeks to safeguard above
all else, whose whole worth consists only in smashing it,
and of which one in our part of the world generally entertains much malicious doubt—and yet to whose preservation
he makes use of very unjust and often loathsome means.
Hence there a woman is always in a prison, whether she
may be a maid, or have a barbaric, good-for-nothing and
always suspicious husband. In the lands of the black,
what better can one expect than what is found prevailing,
namely the feminine sex in the deepest slavery? A de-
spairing man is always a strict master over anyone weaker,
just as with us that man is always a tyrant in the kitchen
who outside his own house hardly dares to look anyone
in the face. Of course, Father Labat reports that a Negro
carpenter, whom he reproached for haughty treatment
toward his wives, answered: "You whites are indeed fools,
for first you make great concessions to your wives, and
afterward you complain when they drive you mad." [6]
And it might be that there were something in this which
perhaps deserved to be considered; but in short, this
fellow was quite black from head to foot, a clear proof
that what he said was stupid. Among all savages there
are none by whom the feminine sex is held in greater
actual regard than by those of Canada. In this they sur-
pass perhaps even our civilized part of the world. Not
as if they paid the women humble respects; those
would be mere compliments. No, they actually exercise

authority. They assemble and deliberate upon the most
important regulations of the nation, even upon the question of war or peace. They thereupon send their deputies
to the men's council and generally it is their voice that
determines the decision. But they purchase this privilege
dearly enough. They are burdened with all the domestic
concerns, and furthermore share all the hardships of the
men.

If, finally, we cast a glance at history, we see the taste
of men, like a Proteus, continually taking on variable
forms. The ancient times of the Greeks and Romans
showed clear indications of a real feeling for the beautiful
as well as for the sublime, in poetry, sculpture, architecture, lawgiving, and even in morals. The sway of the
Roman Caesars changed the noble as well as the beautiful
simplicity into splendor and then into false glitter,
whereof the remnants of their eloquence, poetry, and
even the history of their morals can still inform us.
Gradually even this remainder of a finer taste expired
with the complete decline of the state. The barbarians,
after they in their turn had established their sway, introduced a certain perverted taste called the Gothic, which
discharged itself in the grotesque. Grotesqueries appeared
not merely in the architecture but also in the sciences and
in other practices. The coarsened feeling, once it was
promoted by false art, rather took on every other unnatural [7] form than the ancient simplicity of nature, and
became either exaggerated or trifling. The loftiest flight
that human genius made, in order to ascend to the sub-

lime, took the form of adventures. Spiritual as well as worldly adventures appeared, and oftentimes an obnoxious and monstrous bastardization of both. Monks with the missal in one hand and a war banner in the other were followed by entire armies of deluded victims led to the sacrifice, in order to let their bones be buried in another climate and in a more sacred soil, consecrated warriors sanctified by solemn vows to outrages and misdeeds; and as their sequel, a strange sort of heroic visionaries who called themselves knights and went seeking adventures, tournaments, duels, and fanciful deeds. During that time religion, together with the sciences and morals, became distorted by miserable grotesqueries, and one notes that taste does not easily degenerate in one area without at the same time showing clear signs of its corruption in everything else that belongs to the finer feeling. The monastic vows made out of a great portion of useful men numerous companies of diligent idlers, whose brooding way of life fitted them for hatching out a thousand scholarly grotesqueries, which went thence out into the larger world and spread their kind. Finally, after the human genius has happily raised itself anew from an almost complete destruction by a palingenesis, as it were, in our own days we see the sound taste of the beautiful and noble blossoming forth both in the arts and sciences and in respect to morals. Nothing now is more to be desired than that the false glitter, which so easily deceives, should not remove us unawares from noble simplicity; but especially that the as yet undiscovered secret of education be rescued from the old illusions, in order early to elevate the moral feeling in the breast of every young world-citizen to a lively sensitivity, so that all delicacy of feeling may not amount to merely the fleeting and idle enjoyment of judging, with more or less taste, what goes on around us.

Translator's Notes

Translator's Introduction

[1] *Beobachtungen über das Gefühl des Schönen und Erhabenen* (Königsberg, 1764). The present translation is based on the edition of the Königlich Preussischen Akademie der Wissenschaften in *Kant's Gesammelte Schriften*, Vol. II (Berlin, 1905), pp. 205–256.

[2] J. H. W. Stuckenberg, *The Life of Immanuel Kant* (London, 1882), p. 83.

[3] Johann Gottfried von Herder, *Briefe zu Beförderung der Humanität*, Sechste Sammlung, Brief 79, in *Herders Werke, Deutsche National-Literatur*, ed. Joseph Kürschner (Stuttgart, n.d.), vol. 77, p. 327. Quoted by Stuckenberg, pp. 78–79, whose translation I use.

[4] Herder, *Kritischen Wälder*, in *Herders Sämmtliche Werke*, ed. Bernhard Suphan (Berlin, 1878), IV, 175. My tr.

[5] *Immanuel Kant's Sämmtliche Werke*, ed. G. Hartenstein (Leipzig, 1868), VIII, 625; quoted by Paul Arthur Schilpp, *Kant's Pre-Critical Ethics* (Evanston and Chicago, Northwestern Univ., 1938), p. 73. Schilpp's tr.

[6] Immanuel Kant, *Critique of Pure Reason*, tr. Norman Kemp Smith (New York, Humanities Press, 1950), p. 141.

[7] Page references in this introduction use the pagination of the accompanying translation, and are given in parentheses after each quotation.

[8] Immanuel Kant, *Kant's Cosmogony, as in . . . his Natural History and Theory of the Heavens*, ed. and tr. W. Hastie (Glasgow, Maclehose, 1900), p. 140.

[9] Samuel Holt Monk, *The Sublime: A Study of Critical Theories in XVIII-Century England* (New York, Modern Language Assn., 1935), p. 58.

[10] "General Remark upon the Exposition of the Aesthetical Reflective Judgment," *Critique of Judgment*, tr. J. H. Bernard (New York, Hafner, 1951), pp. 106–120.

[11] Bernard tr., p. 202.

Note on the Translation

[1] Friedrich Paulsen, *Immanuel Kant, His Life and Doctrine*, tr. J. E. Creighton and Alb. Lefevre (London, 1902), p. 403.

[2] G. M. Duncan, "English Translations of Kant's Writings," *Kant-Studien*, II, 253–258.

[3] Bayard Quincy Morgan, *A Critical Bibliography of German Literature in English Translation*, 2d ed. (Stanford Univ., Calif., 1938), p. 257.

[4] René Wellek, *Immanuel Kant in England* (Princeton, 1931), pp. 15–21.

[5] Immanuel Kant, *Critique of Practical Reason and Other Writings in Moral Philosophy*, ed. and tr. Lewis White Beck (Chicago, Univ. of Chicago, 1949), p. vi.

[6] Thomas De Quincey, *Works of Thomas De Quincey*, new and enl. ed. David Masson, 14 vols. (Edinburgh, 1890), XIV, 46-60.

[7] Paul Arthur Schilpp, *Kant's Pre-Critical Ethics* (Evanston and Chicago, Northwestern Univ., 1938), *passim*.

[8] Carl J. Friedrich, *The Philosophy of Kant* (New York, Modern Library, 1949), pp. 3–13.

OBSERVATIONS ON THE FEELING OF THE BEAUTIFUL AND SUBLIME

Section One

[1] Domitian was Roman emperor 81–96 A.D. "At the beginning of his reign he used to spend hours in seclusion every day, doing nothing but catch flies and stab them with a keenly sharpened stylus."—Suetonius, *The Lives of the Caesars*, tr. J. C. Rolfe, rev. (London and New York, 1930), Bk. VIII, Vol. II, p. 345.

[2] Bayle says of Kepler, "We may place him among those authors, who have said, that they valued a production of a mind above a kingdom."—"Kepler," in *The Dictionary Historical and*

Critical of Mr. Peter Bayle, 2d ed. Mr. [Pierre] Des Maizeaux
(London, 1736), III, 659–660.
    ³ *Paradise Lost,* Bk. I.
    ⁴ *Aeneid,* Bk. VI, ll. 637 ff.
    ⁵ *Iliad,* Bk. XIV, ll. 416 ff.
    ⁶ Frederik Hasselquist (1722–1752), a Swedish naturalist,
visited Asia Minor to study the natural history of Palestine,
inspired by Linnaeus, who published Hasselquist's notes five
years after his death in Smyrna. Paul Menzer in the notes to
Vol. II of *Kant's Gesammelte Schriften* locates the citation as
pp. 82–94 of Hasselquist's . . . *Reise nach Palästina in den
Jahren 1749–1752* (Rostock, 1762).
    ⁷ Albrecht von Haller, *Über die Ewigkeit* (1736).

Section Two

    ¹ Traveling as a merchant partner, Jonas Hanway (1712–
1786) of London made his way through Russia and over the
Caspian to the camp of Nadir Shah. He enjoyed the shah's pro-
tection and aid in recovering his goods, whose seizure had caused
him great privation. His journal was published in 1753. Menzer
cites a translation, *Herrn Jonas Hanway zuverlässige Beschreibung*
(Hamburg and Leipzig, 1754), Pt. II, p. 396.
    ² Kant in 1762 had published an essay, "Die falsche Spitz-
findigkeit der vier syllogistischen Figuren" (translated by T. K.
Abbot as "The Mistaken Subtility of the Four Syllogistic Figures"
and published with his translation of *Kant's Introduction to Logic,*
London, 1885), making this point.
    ³ Alceste and Adraste: Though more than one female char-
acter of each name exists in Greek literature, these must be men;
further, they must hold parallel places in literature or history.
Kant is no doubt recalling the Alceste who is Molière's *Misan-
thrope,* and the Adraste who is the hero of that author's *Le
Sicilien ou L'Amour Peintre.* These quotations, however, are not
lines from the plays; they are interpretations of the characters, if
the view suggested is correct. Alceste loves the young widow
madly, but peevishly criticizes her insincere compliments to others.
He is the kind who would be all too aware of her faults as her

charms decline. As *Le Sicilien* is much briefer we do not have as
completely drawn a character; but Adraste, while ardent, is level-
headed, not easily set back by difficulties, cheerful, and apparently
of solid virtue. We would expect him to stand steadfastly by the
wife whom he gains by freeing her from slavery, marching her
confidently past her unwitting master disguised as Adraste's sister.

⁴ This allusion provides interesting evidence of both Kant's
reading tastes and moral bent. The line is from *The Self-Tor-
mentor* of Terence, Act I, scene i, third speech, by Chremes:
"I am a human being; I am interested in everything human. You
may take it that I am giving you this advice . . ."—*The Complete Roman Drama*, ed. George E. Duckworth, 2 vols. (New York,
Random House, 1942), II, 199. Chremes has the character of a
busybody; however, Duckworth adds a note: "This verse became
famous and was often cited by later Roman writers as expressing
the sentiment of the common brotherhood of man."

⁵ In Richardson's novel of 1754, Sir Charles Grandison is
". . . a gentleman of high character and fine appearance . . .
[he] has rendered great services to the noble family of the
Porrettas. . . ." ("Grandison, Sir Charles," *Oxford Companion
to English Literature*, 3d ed. Sir Paul Harvey [Oxford, 1932].)
The triumphs of Robinson [Crusoe] were the taming of goats
and securing of shelter—self-interested, no matter how necessary.

⁶ Though both Catos were known as guardians of the public
morals, the younger Cato of Utica, Caesar's opponent, fits the
context better than his great-grandfather, Cato the Censor. His
character is that of the conscience of Rome and a lover of freedom; after enabling his adherents to escape from Utica by sea,
he committed suicide rather than surrender to the troops of the
unrightful triumvirate. ("Cato . . . , Marcus Porcius of Utica,"
Oxford Companion to Classical Literature, ed. Sir Paul Harvey
[Oxford, 1937].) Plutarch, Lucan, Dante, Montaigne, Hutcheson,
and Addison are among the many authors who preserve his story
with admiration.

⁷ "Ambition" translates *Ehrbegierde*. "Love of honor" in the
previous sentence translates *Ehrliebe*. The similarity of the words
as well as the context shows that Kant refers back to the "sense
of honor" (*Gefühl für Ehre*) introduced on p. 61. It is not a lust
for power or riches, which "ambition" may mean in English, but
a zeal to be thought well of and to be honored by others.

Section Three

¹ Anne Dacier (nee Lefèvre; 1654–1720) translated the *Iliad, Odyssey,* and other Greek and Latin classics into French.

² Voltaire's companion and hostess at Cirey. Her essay on the nature and propagation of fire won a prize in 1738 from the French Academy of Science.

³ Fontenelle's *Entretiens sur la Pluralité des Mondes* (Paris, 1686) purportedly were ladies' conversations about astronomy.

⁴ Francesco, Count Algarotti (1712–1764), a young favorite of Voltaire, wrote *Newtonianismo per le Dame* (1736), an exposition of Newtonian optics, in the manner of Fontenelle especially for women. It proved so popular as to be translated into every European language.

⁵ In his *Allgemeine Naturgeschichte und Theorie des Himmels* (1755), Kant had speculated that the other planets are inhabited, and that the farther from the sun, the lighter are the materials and the more perfect are the structures of their living beings.

⁶ Using "coquette" for *Närrin* and "coxcomb" for the implied word *Narr.* Although a *Närrin* is not always a coquette and a *Narr* is not usually a coxcomb, these translations seem to fit the context and also provide a word "with a changed syllable" to give both masculine and feminine forms.

⁷ No doubt the passage Kant has in mind is in No. 6, by Steele: "When Modesty ceases to be the chief Ornament of one Sex, and Integrity of the other, Society is upon a wrong Basis, and we shall be ever after without Rules to guide our Judgment in what is really becoming and ornamental." (Joseph Addison, Richard Steele, and others, *The Spectator,* 4 vols. [London, Dent; New York, Dutton; 1907], I, 26.) The context as well as the statement is quite relevant.

⁸ *Jungfer.* Literally, "virgin." Also a title of address, like "Miss," used among the bourgeois class in the eighteenth century. Kant undoubtedly intends a pun.

⁹ Ninon de Lenclos (1616–1705) was gay and licentious in youth, later a leader of fashion and a friend of wits and poets.

Her succession of lovers included La Rochefoucauld, Condé, and Saint-Evremond. She left the young Voltaire a bequest to buy books.

[10] The Marchese Giovanni Monaldeschi (d. 1657) was equerry for Christina (1626–1689), queen of Sweden, after she abdicated her throne and sought more adventurous pleasures in Paris and at the French court. There she ordered Monaldeschi assassinated. Whether Kant's suggested reason was the actual one remains unknown.

[11] Lucretia, the heroine of a Roman legend and of works by Chaucer, Gower, and Shakespeare, suffered outrage; having revealed the fact to her husband, she took her own life.

[12] "Every nation has ideas of beauty peculiar to itself; and every individual has his own notions and taste concerning that quality. These peculiarities probably originate from the first agreeable impressions we receive of certain objects; and therefore depend more upon chance and habit than upon difference of constitution."—Georges Louis Leclerc, Comte de Buffon, *Natural History, General and Particular,* tr. Wm. Smellie, ed. Wm. Wood, 20 vols. (London, 1812), III, 203.

Section Four

[1] Apparently Kant had ample opportunity for experience on which to base such generalizations. His biographer Stuckenberg describes the eighteenth-century population of Königsberg as extremely diversified, having Polish, Russian, Scandinavian, Dutch, and English segments, in addition to the predominating German and earlier Slavic portions. Not only commercial interests of the port but also the military garrison and the university brought intellectually stimulating persons to the city. (J. H. W. Stuckenberg, *The Life of Immanuel Kant* [London, 1882], pp. 2–4.)

[2] The San Benito was a scapular, a loose, sleeveless monastic garment introduced by St. Benedict. That worn by confessed heretics was yellow and was decorated with flames and figures of devils.

[3] Kant has indicated the cognates from Latin for these terms

in parentheses in the original: *"Leichtgläubigkeit (Credulität),
Aberglaube (Superstition), Schwärmerei (Fanaticism), und
Gleichgültigkeit (Indifferentism)."*

⁴ In a note to his essay "Of National Characters," Hume
says: "I am apt to suspect the Negroes to be naturally inferior
to the Whites. There scarcely ever was a civilized nation of that
complexion, nor even any individual, eminent either in action or
speculation. No ingenious manufactures amongst them, no arts,
no sciences. On the other hand, the most rude and barbarous of
the Whites, such as the ancient Germans, the present Tartars,
have still something eminent about them, in their valour, form
of government, or some other particular. Such a uniform and
constant difference could not happen, in so many countries and
ages, if nature had not made an original distinction between these
breeds of men. Not to mention our colonies, there are Negro
slaves dispersed all over Europe, of whom none ever discovered
any symptoms of ingenuity; though low people, without education, will start up amongst us, and distinguish themselves in every
profession. In Jamaica, indeed, they talk of one Negro as a man
of parts and learning; but it is likely he is admired for slender
accomplishments, like a parrot who speaks a few words plainly."
—David Hume, *Essays and Treatises on Several Subjects,* 2 vols.
(Edinburgh, 1825), I, 521–522. "Of National Characters" was
first published in 1748.

⁵ Attakullaculla was an able Cherokee chieftain, one of
seven that Sir Alexander Cuming in 1730 brought to England,
where the daily newspapers occasionally carried descriptions and
stories of the visit of these savages to civilization. A coincidence
probably unknown to Kant was that not a native Lycurgus but
Cuming was declared lawgiver, and a chief, of the Cherokees.
He was, however, shortly exposed as a swindler of colonists and
fell into debt and dishonor. Attakullaculla upon returning re-
sumed an eminent career as leader and peacemaker, befriending
and preserving the life of an English captain after the noble
fashion Kant admired. ("Attakullaculla," *Handbook of American
Indians North of Mexico,* Smithsonian Institution, Bureau of
American Ethnology, Bulletin 30 [Washington, 1907], Pt. I,
p. 115. Also "Cuming or Cumming, Sir Alexander," *Dictionary*

of National Biography [London, 1888].) In the text, Kant's spelling of the Indian name has been preserved.

⁶ Jean Baptiste Labat (1663–1738), a Dominican, published some nineteen volumes of his travels during and after his years as a missionary in the West Indies. Menzer in the notes in *Kant's Gesammelte Schriften,* Vol. II, locates this incident in Labat's *Voyage du père Labat aux îles de l'Amérique* (Haye, 1724), II, 54.

⁷ Reading *unnatürliche* with Cassirer (*Immanuel Kants Werke* [Berlin, Cassirer, 1922] II, 299); *Akademie* edition gives *natürliche.* In the *Lesarten* of the Cassirer edition, *natürliche* is called a printer's error that the *Akademie* edition retains from the second (1766) edition.